OCEANSIDE

Photo Researcher: John Daley
Produced in cooperation with the
Oceanside Historical Society
Windsor Publications, Inc.
Northridge, California

OCEANSIDE

CREST OF THE WAVE

Windsor Publications, Inc.—History Books
Division

Managing Editor: Karen Story

Design Director: Alexander D'Anca

Staff for *Oceanside: Crest of the Wave*

Senior Editor: Pamela Schroeder

Photo Editor: Cameron Cox

Text Production Editor: Doreen Nakakihara

Editor, Corporate Biographies: Alyson Gould

Production Editor, Corporate Biographies: Albert
Polito·

Senior Proofreader: Susan J. Muhler

Editorial Assistants: Didier Beauvoir, Thelma
Fleischer, Suzanne Kelley, Kim Kievman, Rebecca
Kropp, Michael Nugwynne, Kathy B. Peyser, Pat
Pittman, Theresa J. Solis

Sales Representative, Corporate Biographies: Merl
Wolfgang

Designer: Tanya Maiboroda

Layout Artist: Dan Irwin

Layout Artist, Corporate Biographies: Barbara
Moore

Library of Congress Cataloging-in-Publication Data
Sully, Langdon.
    Oceanside: crest of the wave/Langdon Sully.—
    1st ed.
    p. 128 cm. 22 x 28
    Bibliography: p. 125
    Includes index.
    ISBN 0-89781-282-4
    1. Oceanside (Calif.)—History. 2. Oceanside
(Calif.)—Description—Views. 3. Oceanside
(Calif.)—Industries. I. Title.
F869.027S85 1988
979.4'98—dc19   88-27892
                                          CIP

Windsor Publications, Inc.
Elliot Martin, Chairman of the Board
James L. Fish III, Chief Operating Officer

Title page: *The sun setting over the
Pacific silhouettes the Oceanside pier.
Photo by Stephen Whalen. Courtesy,
Zephyr Pictures*

CONTENTS

*The Rosicrucian Fellowship was
founded in 1911 by Max Heindel.
Pictured here, the Rosicrucian Healing
Temple was dedicated on Christmas
Eve 1920. Photo by Joseph M. Daley*

PREFACE

The most important—and the most time-consuming—part of any historian's work is the research. A day's intensive digging may turn up as only a few paragraphs in the finished manuscript. In writing this book, I was fortunate enough to work with a research team made up of members of the Oceanside Historical Society. They put in countless hours to provide me with books, newspaper clippings, writings, interviews, and letters, without which it would not have been possible to produce this book. I am deeply indebted to Bette and Wic Burgeson (he is past president of the Oceanside Historical Society and co-ordinated the research). I am most grateful also to John Daley, current president of the Oceanside Historical Society, who was a wizard at coming up with that special piece of information when I needed it yesterday, and who sorted through mountains of photographs, ancient and recent, to pick the best of the best. I can't say enough about Kristi S. Pippert, archivist of the Oceanside Historical Society, for her prodigious effort in converting almost unreadable microfilm into easy-to-work-with typewritten notes. Thanks also to former mayor Howard Richardson, Paul B. Beck, Edith Swaim, Bill Atwell, and Ernest A. Taylor, who have served the City of Oceanside in many capacities.

—Langdon Sully

Oceanside's image has always included a pier, and residents are justly proud and pleased that their "trademark" has been so beautifully enhanced and re-created. Photo by Stephen Whalen. Courtesy, Zephyr Pictures

CHAPTER **1**

THE
LAND OF
MISSION
SAN LUIS
REY

The first residents of northern San Diego County were hunter-gatherers, who carved a living from the land and the waters that met at the future site of Oceanside. Long before the first white explorers sailed up the coast and long before the Spanish named the river valley San Luis Rey and the natives Luisenos, the fertile soil was dotted with Indian villages and footpaths. One village is known to have existed just east of present-day Whelan Lake, the Indians' *ramadas* and lean-tos situated north of the river about five miles from the coast. The Luisenos called the pretty stream nearby the *Keish.*

These people were from the Shoshone Indian families usually associated with the vast plains and deserts of Nevada and Utah. They were, for the most part, more adaptable and more religious than their neighbors, the Yumans, to the south. Neither wanderers nor farmers, the Luisenos enjoyed a much more varied subsistence life-style than did most other Indians of Southern California. Their environment stretched from the upper reaches of Mount Palomar through rolling hills to the coast,

These Luisenos are seen working at their home in the San Luis Rey Valley sometime around 1890. Their residence is a reflection of the Franciscan influence so dominant during the eighteenth and nineteenth centuries. Friars from the mission taught the Indians how to build homes, farm the land, and raise livestock. Courtesy, Oceanside Historical Society

Seen here in an image from 1884, these Indians relax in front of a typical "ramada." Courtesy, Southwest Museum, Los Angeles

allowing them access to the rich forests of the mountains as well as to the lush grasslands, streams, and marshes that stretched down through the valleys to the Pacific Ocean.

The Luisenos lived in temporary villages in thatched conical huts, which were partly underground. These dwellings were usually clustered around a ceremonial structure, called the *wamkis,* where important tribal rituals took place. Another type of subterranean hut, the *temescal,* or sweathouse, was used by the men for ritual cleansing of their bodies.

Rectangular, thatched structures, later known as *ramadas,* were used for daily domestic chores. And it was here that the Luisenos particularly excelled. Their pottery and basketry are considered among the finest of all the California Indians. Their wonderful baskets were crafted with grass stems wound with rush or sumac. Beautiful designs were created by varying the color of the grass or by adding pine

needles or trinkets. They were the only California Indians to make a clothlike textile, which was woven of nettle fiber, milkweed, and mescal.

The Indians generally located their villages near a reliable source of water. The water was needed to prepare their primary source of food—the acorn. The women would crush the acorns, leach them in water to remove the bitterness, then grind them into a flour-like mixture called *weewish.* Most of the village would travel to the mountains in the fall to gather acorns and hunt for local game, including deer, rabbits, rats, mice, antelope, and various birds and fowl. The men also fished the streams and hunted sea mammals, crab, and abalone along the coast. These staples were supplemented with grubs, grasshoppers, grasses, greens, cactus pods and fruit, wild berries and bulbs, mushrooms, and tree fungi. Teas were brewed for pleasure and for medicinal purposes.

Because temperatures were generally mild—ranging from 52 to 68 degrees along the coast and from 40 to 85 degrees inland—the Indians required very little clothing. In cooler temperatures they would wear robes made from the skins of deer, otters, or rabbits. Women wore aprons made from cedar bark. Personal ornaments and body painting were important for social and religious functions.

There were at least 10,000 Shoshones living in and around the future site of Oceanside when the first Anglos arrived. But the number of Indians began to drop off precipitously from disease and unsanitary living conditions as soon as the Spanish marched onto the scene.

Although European explorers, starting in 1542 with Juan Rodrigues Cabrillo, sailed past the hills of San Luis Rey, it was not until 1769 that Spain launched its quest to conquer Alta (Upper) California. That year the Portola Expedition sailed into San Diego Bay. The president of the prospective Alta California missions, Father Junipero Serra, and Don Gaspar de Portola, the governor of Baja (Lower) California, launched what would be more than 60 years of Catholic domination of Alta California.

The Franciscans eventually built a network of 21 missions, spaced about 30 miles, or one day's travel, apart from each other from San Diego north. The San Diego mission was the first, founded in 1769. But 16 additional missions were built north of San Diego before the need for a mission halfway between the Mission San Diego de Alcala and the Mission San Juan Capistrano, founded in 1776, could be fulfilled.

On June 13, 1798, Father Fermin Francisco de Lasuen, who had succeeded Father Serra as mission presi-

dent, founded Mission San Luis Rey de Francia on its present site in the valley—on an elevation with a commanding position, near but not on the ocean, with fertile fields and water available for irrigation. The mission was named in honor of Louis IX, the king of France, who had been a Franciscan himself. San Luis Rey was the 18th mission in the chain and would eventually become the largest, the most populous, and the most prosperous of all the missions in Califor-

A Luiseno Indian proudly displays his fine basket. The Luiseno Indians were the first inhabitants of the San Luis Rey Valley. Like many Indian tribes they had no name for themselves. The Franciscans who founded the Mission San Luis Rey in 1798 originally called the Indians "San Luisenos." They later shortened that to "Luisenos." Courtesy, Southwest Museum, Los Angeles

nia. On its very first day, 54 children were baptized. Nineteen young adult Indians also wanted to be baptized, but were told they would have to attend Catechism first.

Much of the mission's success is attributed to Father Antonio Peyri, whose industry and intelligence guided the community for 33 years. The only assistance Father Peyri had in the beginning came from a handful of soldiers from the San Diego presidio and a few Indian neophytes from the Mission San Juan Capistrano. The dauntless party began to work with only "a few pickaxes, a dozen ploughshares, half a dozen crowbars, some blankets, a quantity of flannel, and two dozen bolts of cloth to clothe the naked Indians," according to an account left by the Reverend Domingo Rivas.

Father Antonio Peyri was assigned to San Luis Rey and served as its administrator for 34 years, supervising the building program and the largest Indian population of the province. Courtesy, Oceanside Historical Society

Father Peyri was the architect and directed operations while the soldiers became builders and the Indians became laborers. Within weeks, the Luisenos were taught how to make adobe brick and how to hew timbers out of rough logs. The timbers for the mission were 25 feet tall and 20 inches square and they were carried on the backs of the Indians in five-mile relays from Mount Palomar, some 28 miles away. Once they were hefted onto the Indians' shoulders, the timbers were sprinkled with holy water and the bearers admonished that the timbers would be desecrated if they touched the ground.

The mission itself was the largest and one of the most beautiful in all of California. It was laid out in a vast quadrangle, measuring 630 by 550 feet. By 1802 an adobe church large enough for 1,000 Indians had been completed. Four rooms built of adobe and roofed with tiles made on the spot had been erected for use as granaries. The next three years saw the building of an apartment for girls and unmarried women, two large tanks for tanning hide, and a boiler for making soap. A guardhouse and homes for the guards, corrals, and other outbuildings soon appeared on the landscape. The present San Luis Rey chapel was in the planning stages in 1811. Construction of the church was completed four years later and the present-day church at Mission San Luis Rey, the King of the Missions, was dedicated on October 4, 1815.

The Indians were given food, clothing, and shelter and were taught how to farm and to raise cattle as well as trained at various trades. The Indians prepared the fields around the mission for planting and raised the crops. They dug ditches and built aqueducts for baths and laundry facilities and to carry the water to the fields to nourish the growth. They familiarized the padres with certain foods that grew nearby, showed them where to hunt, and taught them how to use fish traps and to build small boats. The Indians were natural *vaqueros* and the men made leather out of the hides of cattle. The women were weavers and produced textiles and baskets; they made soap and candles out of tallow. The children learned to play musical instruments and to sing religious songs in church.

There are some who hold that the Indians were driven to their accomplishments through fear and punishment. It was true that the Luisenos were prohibited from leaving the mission and were held there as virtual serfs. Indians who attempted to leave the missions were chased down and recaptured by soldiers, who often returned with new, forced conscripts. Yet it seems clear that Father Peyri felt great affection for his wards as reflected by a traveler, Auguste Duhaut-Cilly, who visited in 1827:

Truly, his mission was that, of all California, where these poor people were the best treated. Not only were they well fed and clothed; but still more, he gave them some money on feast days. Every Saturday he distributed soap among the women. On this occasion, all passed before him, while the padre spoke to each in turn. He knew them all: he praised one, mildly reproached another; to this one a joke befitting the occasion, to that a fatherly reproof: all went away satisfied or touched.

Above: W.R. Hutton arrived in Oceanside from Washington, D.C., and worked as a surveyor and draftsman at the time of this drawing. Hutton's sketch documents the Mission San Luis Rey in 1848 when it was the longest building in California. Courtesy, Oceanside Historical Society

Left: At the time of this photograph, sometime in 1895, the combined age of these Indian women exceeded 300 years. The women lived near the San Luis Rey mission and survived chiefly by begging. Courtesy, Oceanside Historical Society

By 1831 the mission population had swollen to 3,000 Indians, making it California's most populous mission. Perhaps because the padres controlled the local economy, many Indians felt it left them little alternative but to join the Christianized community.

Because of this large, captive work force, the holdings of the Mission San Luis Rey eventually spread across what would become six large ranchos, with thousands of acres of grazing and agricultural land. The livestock herd had been started with only a few cows, horses, and mules donated by the missions at San Diego and San Juan Capistrano. At the peak of its glory, San Luis Rey raised more livestock than any other mission and was second only to the Mission San Gabriel in the production of grain. Production peaked at some 27,000 head of cattle, 26,100 sheep, 1,300 goats, 300 pigs, 1,950 horses, and 180 mules. It produced as much as 67,000 bushels of grain in a single year. It is no wonder the missions captured the eyes of soldiers and adventurers, who longed for a cut of the wealth.

The Franciscans claimed, however, that the land was the property of the Indians, to be held in trust for them for 10 years or until they should become civilized and qualified for ownership; the military maintained that the land belonged to the Spanish Crown. The situation came to a head in 1821 when Mexico declared itself to be independent of Spain. The Crown was already supporting wars at home and in Latin America and saw little alternative but to relinquish its claim to California. That put Mexican military forces in control, thus assuring that the demise of the mission system was only a matter of time.

When it became painfully evident that the missions would lose their holdings, Father Peyri left the mission in 1832. Knowing that his Indians would try to stop him from going, he left in the dead of night. Legend has it that 500 of them, learning of his departure, mounted their horses and rode to San Diego to intercept him. But when they reached the shore, it was only in time to see him board his ship. Some dove into the water to try to reach him; but the ship was already under way.

Father Peyri took two young Indians away with him. Agapitus Amamix and Pablo Tac had shown great promise at the mission school and the padre brought them to Rome to study for the priesthood. Amamix died in 1837. Tac did very well in his studies—writing poetry, his recollections of early Luiseno life, and beginning a dictionary of the Luiseno lanuage. But he, too, died in 1841, at the age of 19. His writings, however, are believed to be the first by a native Californian.

In 1834 forced secularization—or confiscation—took place. It was the single most important event in the Mexican era. Ironically it was the mission accomplishments—showing that the land could support crops and livestock necessary for survival, the establishment of lines of communication, and the effective subordination of the Indians—that convinced the Mexicans they could no longer tolerate church domination of all this potential wealth.

When the Mission San Luis Rey was turned over to Mexican military authorities, they began to turn over plots of land to individual Indians. But life under the padres had not prepared the Luisenos to oversee the ranchos. The Indians had been given their "freedom" in 1826 and the result was much the same as that stemming

from the freedom of the slaves after the Civil War. The Luisenos were accustomed to following the orders of the padres. Even though the Indians were given land, they frequently lost it before they even occupied it—selling it off, trading it for whiskey or trifles, or being cheated out of it by dishonest administrators.

The Luisenos saw their mission being plundered and looted and falling into ruins for want of care. They watched the once-fertile fields turn to weeds and their cattle being slaughtered for the hides. Poverty drove some Luisenos to a life of crime. Others fled inland in a vain attempt to resume their tribal lifestyle. But many were grateful to find work on the ranchos that dotted the valley. For many

of the Indians, secularization simply meant they'd exchanged one system of servitude for another.

The ranchos would take over the the missions in the 1830s as the dominant force in Alta California. At the beginning of the Mexican era there were about two dozen huge ranchos, but by the time the Americans took over in 1846 and 1847, those had been broken down into hundreds. And the abundance of cheap labor encouraged the landowners to maintain an easy and much-storied lifestyle.

The hide and tallow trade boomed following secularization in 1834 until the American takeover 12 years later. After that a dwindling market in the East, as well as several years of

In 1832 Father Peyri left the mission in the dead of the night. Legend has it that 500 Indians tried to intercept him only to see him pull away from the shores of San Diego. Courtesy, Oceanside Historical Society

Born in San Gabriel in 1801, Pio Pico moved to San Diego in 1829 where he operated a grog shop. On May 10, 1841, the Ranchos San Onofre y Santa Margarita, consisting of 89,742 acres, were given to Pio Pico and his brother Andres by California Governor Alvarado. The Picos then obtained Rancho Los Flores by first granting the land in the name of an Indian, and then transferring title to themselves. A successful rancher and businessman, Pico would become the last Mexican governor of California, taking office on February 22, 1845. Courtesy, Oceanside Historical Society

drought, brought that trade to its knees. The short-sightedness of the rancho families was also to blame. They ignored the possibility of gold and ore in the mountains inland, and even though they oversaw vast tracts of land and thousands of head of cattle, for the most part they showed no interest in farming or in dairying. They also became dependent on the manufactured goods that the often-illicit Yankee traders carried into California ports and later across overland trails.

Of the 20 San Diego County ranchos for which government patents were issued, three ranchos—previously under the jurisdiction of the Mission San Luis Rey—were important to the history of Oceanside. One was Santa Margarita y Las Flores (which stretched from Oceanside into Riverside and Orange counties), the largest and most prized of all the ranchos. The rancho had 133,440 acres, including 18 miles of coastline, 3 mountain ranges, several lakes, 5 rivers, and 260 miles of roads—a holding one-fourth the size of the State of Rhode Island. It was stocked with 15,000 sheep, 10,000 cattle, and 2,000 horses.

When the Mexican government began giving away the mission lands, the Rancho Santa Margarita, just north of present-day Oceanside, was snapped up by the Pico brothers, Pio and Andres. Pio Pico had been administrator of the San Luis Rey Mission following its secularization and this alone gave him the inside track. But the brothers were also active in efforts to secure California for Mexico, and were among the men rewarded for their efforts by the government. Pio Pico was twice governor of California during the Mexican era and Andres would become a general

in the Mexican army. Many of their friends and relatives would also benefit from the Picos' unscrupulous land grabbing.

The Picos were granted title to the Rancho Santa Margarita in 1841. Three years later they were conspiring to acquire the adjoining Rancho Las Flores. The Picos felt that if they applied for the grant in their own names, its validity might be questioned. So they granted the Rancho Las Flores to Jose Manuel, one of the Indians living in the starving pueblo at Las Flores. They then transferred title to themselves.

Santa Margarita y Las Flores prospered for a time under the Picos. But Andres was more interested in the military and sold his share to his brother for $1,000. Pio Pico was careless about money matters and an

Pio Pico sold Rancho Santa Margarita to his brother-in-law, Don Juan Forster, in 1864. In an effort to regain the land, Pico sued Forster in 1872 over title to Santa Margarita. The trial lasted for weeks but it took only 20 minutes for the jury to decide in Forster's favor. Forster was one of the largest land holders in California. He died at the ranch February 20, 1882. Courtesy, Oceanside Historical Society

inveterate gambler and sold the rancho to his brother-in-law, Juan Forster (an Englishman who had settled in San Juan Capistrano), in 1864 for $14,000. Although Forster was a very wealthy man, living at Santa Margarita in regal style, he dissipated his fortune, had to borrow $207,000 on the rancho from Charles Crocker of San Francisco, and died virtually penniless. Upon Forster's death, the rancho changed hands twice more. Then, in 1942, it was sold to the United States Navy for a Marine Corps base, named Camp Pendleton. This base would have a profound effect on the history of Oceanside.

Another prominent Mexican clan gained title to the Agua Hedionda Rancho, 13,311 acres on the south side of present-day Oceanside. In 1842 this tract went to Don Juan Maria Marron, a prominent San Diegan. He married Dona Felipa, the daughter of Juan Maria Osuna, the first alcalde at San Diego. During the Mexican War, Juan Maria Marron suffered considerably because of his support of the Americans against the wishes of his Mexican friends. In 1846 a band of his fellow Californios arrested him. They let him go, but stripped the Agua Hedionda Rancho of its horses and cattle. The Marron family built several adobe homes on the rancho over the years. One was built by Juan Maria Marron, the grandson of the original grantee. It sat on the north side of today's Highway 78, about a mile east of the El Camino Real (where the Southern California Auto Club is now located). The adobe was in ruins in 1968 with only a few walls still standing.

Rancho Guajome, a tract of 2,219 acres, was also on Mission San Luis Rey land east of the mission complex. Pio Pico granted it to two Indians of

the mission on July 19, 1845, but they soon lost the grant. Ultimately, Colonel Cave Johnson Couts gained title in the early 1850s, and it stayed in the family until 1943. Rancho Guajome is now a San Diego County Regional Park, consisting of about 565 acres: 400 acres in Oceanside and 165 acres in Vista.

American and Mexican soldiers began streaming through San Luis Rey in the mid-1840s as the two countries fought for supremacy. John Charles Fremont took possession of San Luis Rey in August 1846. General Stephen W. Kearny, his guide, Kit Carson, and 100 U.S. dragoons camped at San Luis Rey in December 1846. This was also the year that American settlers in Sacramento staged the Bear Flag Revolt, declaring California a part of the United States. But the struggle continued until January 13, 1847, when Mexico signed the Treaty of Capitulation at Cahuenga Pass, and the land that would become Oceanside changed hands once again.

Ten days later the Mormon Battalion straggled into San Luis Rey, the weary men catching their first sight of the sparkling Pacific, after their historic journey from Council Bluffs, Iowa, on their way to their final destination, San Diego. The next month these volunteer soldiers were sent back to San Luis Rey to clean up and repair the mission complex. Among the volunteers was Jean-Baptiste Charbonneau. Half-Indian, half-white, he had been born on the Lewis and Clark Expedition, the son of its chief guide, Toussaint Charbonneau, and Sacajawea.

The younger Charbonneau was a guide for the Mormon Battalion, and he and some 500 other adventurers expected to be paid for their efforts by being allowed to resettle in California. Jean-Baptiste opted to remain in the Oceanside area and in 1847 was appointed to the position of alcalde at San Luis Rey. A pitiful array of Indians still at the mission fell under this jurisdiction. Among them was an Indian named Fulgencio.

After he was freed by Mexican authorities, Fulgencio was employed as a laborer for 12 1/2 cents a day. Those wages were payable in trade at the Jose Antonio Pico general store in San Luis Rey. Fulgencio ran up a bill, however, mostly for wine and whiskey, that he could never hope to cover with his wages. But Jose Pico demanded payment, and Jean-Baptiste Charbonneau was forced to order Fulgencio to work off a debt of $51.37 at the rate of 12 1/2 cents a day.

Charbonneau resigned from his post in 1848, saying the settlers seemed to feel that his Indian blood made him favor the Indians too much. More likely he could not tolerate the thought of condemning his fellow Indians to virtual slavery for piling up debts through behavior the white men had taught them.

Although the mission was returned to the Franciscans in 1843, considering its state of disrepair, there was little the padres could do to help the few hundred Indians who remained. San Luis Rey ceased to be a mission in 1846, when Governor Pio Pico sold it for $2,437. Over time the mission was thoroughly plundered by soldiers, travelers, and the local ranchers, who stripped it of all useful building materials and many of its treasures.

The mission was used to garrison U.S. troops or was ignored until the United States court declared the sale of the land illegal and a portion of the lands was returned to the church. This act was formalized on March 18, 1865, when President Abraham Lincoln, just a month before his assassination, signed the deed that returned the lands to the mission. But the mission would fall into neglect for another quarter-century before the Franciscans returned to reclaim their handiwork.

This unusual photograph from the rear of the Mission San Luis Rey reveals the total decay of the sacristy. On the left, the open dome of the mortuary chapel shows the amount of destruction and neglect which occurred after secularization. Courtesy, Seaver Center for Western History Research. Natural History Museum of Los Angeles County

CHAPTER **2**

THE BEGINNINGS OF A COASTAL TOWN

Lieutenant Cave Johnson Couts arrived at Mission San Luis Rey with the army in April 1849. A seasoned soldier and frontiersman, Couts kept a detailed record of his roamings. He wrote of the valley as though he had found his promised land. Water, according to Couts' diary, was "abundant and good. Several springs meet at the creek, which runs into the Pacific about four and a half miles from the mission." Couts noted the chain of mountains to the north was covered with wild oats. And he described the valley as "unsurpassed by any other in the country." Couts also noted the effects of the Gold Rush, writing, "Naked and shirttailed Indians and Mexicans or Californians, go and return in 15 or 20 days with over a pound of pure gold each, per day." In light of the mineral wealth the U.S. government wasted little time in securing its claim to California, making it a state in 1850.

Cave Johnson Couts was born in Tennessee in 1821, a nephew of Cave Johnson, who served as secretary of the treasury under President James K. Polk. Couts graduated from West Point and served on the frontier through the Mexican War. But after

These beachgoers, in a photo from 1887, enjoy a day at the beach. Seen in the picture is Oceanside Beach looking north from the site of today's Oceanside Pier. The bathhouse on the right sits where the present Community Center is now located. Courtesy, San Diego Historical Society-Ticor Collection

seeing the San Luis Rey Valley, Couts set his mind on making it his home. The tall, handsome soldier wooed and won the hand of Dona Ysidora Bandini, daughter of one of the wealthiest and most powerful of the Spanish Dons. They married in 1851 at the family adobe in San Diego's Old Town. Shortly after the wedding, Couts took his bride to show her the place he wanted to live. It was Rancho Guajome. The rancho belonged to Dona Ysidora's brother-in-law, Abel Stearns, a Los Angeles trader and moneylender. The land was deeded to the Couts as a wedding gift.

Couts moved his wife and first two children to Rancho Guajome in 1853, making him the first white settler of San Luis Rey. He was a meticulous businessman and raised thousands of head of cattle and other livestock. During the Gold Rush, Couts risked his neck on cattle drives north to San Francisco, where he could command a better price. Unlike most of the Dons, he recognized the agricultural potential of the land. He irrigated and planted extensive orchards. With his profits, Couts bought up additional land and oversaw the building of his beloved Rancho Guajome. He used his authority as sub-Indian agent to make sure he had enough workers.

There were still several hundred Luisenos scratching out an existence in and around Mission San Luis Rey in the 1850s. Many of them were descendants of the original builders. From this pool Couts hired laborers for almost nothing to build a 20-room adobe mansion on a rise just south of the current Vista city limits. Much of the building material came from the abandoned mission, a distance of about four miles. The bishop offered the huge roof beams and adobe tiles to the ranchers in return for a donation to the diocese.

Over the next two decades Couts added barns, stables, sheds, corrals, servants quarters, and a chapel to Rancho Guajome. It was in this setting that Helen Hunt Jackson collected material for her famous protest about the fate of the California Indians. Called *Ramona*, the story was published in 1884. A play based on the book is still performed annually to large audiences in Hemet. The Rancho Guajome house today is a monument to the glory days of the Dons.

Couts maintained a grand style of living at Rancho Guajome. He held a number of civic and judicial titles, and was appointed a colonel and aide-de-camp to California governor John Bigler, who took office in 1852. But Couts was also known for having a fiery temper and sometimes taking the law into his own hands. In 1855 Couts was indicted twice for beating the Indians who were building Rancho Guajome. The cases never went to trial, but rumors of such mistreatment resulted in his dismissal as sub-Indian agent. Couts faced indictment on a number of occasions, the charges ranging from land swindling to attempted murder, but he was never convicted.

Despite Colonel Couts' notoriety, he wielded great authority and was highly respected in San Diego County. Although he never lived to see the founding of Oceanside, he is counted among its forefathers who pioneered in the San Luis Rey Valley. It was here that Oceanside's first white settlement sprang up in the 1860s and 1870s.

After the sale of Mission San Luis Rey land was declared illegal and some property formally returned to the church in 1865, the pattern of land ownership in the valley changed drastically. Only a fraction of the mission's original holdings were actually returned to the church and the rest fell under the jurisdiction of the new state government. Within two years a new breed of pioneer would start taking up homesteads around the valley. These settlers came from as far away as Europe and Australia, as well as from North America, attracted by the

The Rancho Guajome originally contained 2,219 acres and was given by Able Stearns to Colonel Cave J. Couts as a wedding present. Couts soon built, with Indian labor, a ranch house that contained 20 rooms, a patio, warehouses, stables, a chapel, and servants quarters. The lovely setting supposedly inspired author Helen Hunt Jackson to write the novel Ramona *while a guest at the rancho. Courtesy, San Diego Historical Society-Ticor Collection*

beauty and potential of the sunny San Luis Rey Valley.

The first settlers arrived in the late 1860s. By 1870 there were seven families living in the San Luis Rey Valley. Heads of the households were Benjamin Franklin Libby, D.R. Foss, John Adams, P.A. Graham, Herbert Crouch, Major Lee H. Utt, and James M. Griffin. It was a rugged existence. There were few amenities, and many families had to fight in the courts for years to secure their claims to homestead lands.

Most of the settlers took up farming or ranching in the isolated valley. Herbert Crouch was a "Sixty-Niner," and one of the earliest to settle the valley. Crouch teamed up with Major Lee Utt in a sheep venture. They imported Merino sheep, renowned for their fine, white fleece. When the partners sold out in 1887, their sheep were considered among the nation's finest. Benjamin Franklin Libby, a native of Maine, took up homestead land and eventually had a 300-acre dairy, stock, and alfalfa ranch. James Griffin worked as a farmer, a tradition his son, John Griffin, carried on in the valley. John developed a passion for horses and the descendants of his original stock were prized for decades to come. He gained prominence later on the San Diego County Board of Supervisors. B.F. Hubbert owned one of the largest (600 acres) and most fruitful ranches around Oceanside. Public-spirited and energetic, he eventually served as constable for Oceanside.

Commercial establishments in the valley were slower to arrive. Simon Goldbaum, a native of Prussia, set up his first general store in the valley in 1872. It was situated northwest of the mission, where the village of San Luis Rey would sprout. He and his brothers eventually owned several stores there and in Oceanside. But in the early days money was frequently scarce and many of the settlers were forced to live off what they could grow on their own.

Compounding the difficulties of life on the frontier, the drought years in the early 1870s depressed the San Luis Rey area. Some of the early settlers left. By 1874 sheep ranching was replacing cattle ranching as the dominant industry around San Luis Rey. But the transition was anything but

Herbert Crouch and his wife, Martha Avenell, settled in the San Luis Rey Valley in 1869. Crouch raised sheep and later began harvesting grain on more than 1,800 acres of land. Courtesy, Oceanside Historical Society

Above: Benjamin Franklin Libby came with his family to San Luis Rey in 1867. They were some of the Valley's original settlers. Shown here in an image from the 1880s are, from left to right, B.F. Libby, Grace, Margaret Stone Libby, Emma, Anne, and Katherine. Courtesy, Oceanside Historical Society

Left: B.F. "Uncle Ben" Hubbert, shown here on horseback, came to the San Luis Rey Valley with his parents in 1873 when he was 13 years old. He had a 600-acre ranch near Oceanside, and for over 16 years served as the constable. Courtesy, Oceanside Historical Society

Andrew Jackson Myers, the founder of Oceanside, was born in Illinois on April 10, 1840. He came to California in 1877 and soon settled in the San Luis Rey Township. In 1883 he applied for a land grant and was awarded 160 acres, thus creating Oceanside's original townsite. Among his many contributions to Oceanside were the city's first water works and land he donated for the Christian Church. Courtesy, Oceanside Historical Society

backs before he died in 1874. The loyal Dona Ysidora maintained the ranchos until her death in 1897. Then her son, Cave Johnson Couts, Jr., proudly took over and was known as the "last of the Dons." He maintained Rancho Guajome in typical Californio style until he died on July 15, 1943, in the same room and same bed in which he had been born in 1856.

During the 1880s the trickle of settlers into the Oceanside area would become a stream. The waters were pushed along by the Balfor, Guthrie Land & Town Company, which in 1879 began promoting land in Southern California. The company sent out colorful brochures, advertising the San Luis Rey area—its fertile soil, healthy climate, and spectacular countryside. The firm suggested that San Luis Rey offered an easy life (probably stressing little or no work—everything grew without tending) and included drawings of ships on the San Luis Rey River. This in spite of the fact that the water was not deep enough for a ship of any size; moreover, not long after distribution of the brochures, a bridge was built across the river and the pilings made passage impossible.

Although San Luis Rey would eventually have all the makings of a frontier town—with its own hotel, livery stable, telegraph station, post office, and stagecoach line—it was destined to be overshadowed by the upstart along the coast. In 1887 there were about 600 people living in the valley. Many would eventually move to Oceanside. But the San Luis Rey settlement, today a part of Oceanside, is commemorated by Heritage Park, a cluster of historic buildings, including the original building of the *Oceanside Blade*, the Libby School, moved in

peaceful. It precipitated a range war. The sheepmen, as well as the growing number of farmers, fenced in the land, taking grazing range away from the free-roaming cattle. Herbert Crouch remembered several instances of haystacks being burned and pistols being drawn. San Luis Rey's only lynching took place in the heat of this battle. The emotions were running high when a military deserter known as "Friday" Blanchard was accused of shooting a local rancher. Blanchard was summarily punished by a mob of angry residents.

The combination of the range war, the drought, and a smallpox epidemic forced Cave Couts to sell off many of his cattle for a pittance. He never fully recovered financially from these set-from across the river, and the first concrete jail built in Oceanside. All Saints Church, built in 1890, still stands near the site of the old San Luis Rey settlement.

The two men who really put Oceanside on the map were living at San Luis Rey when they realized the new railroad would be passing below them, along the coast. Andrew Jackson Myers started life in La Salle, Illinois, in 1840. Myers' father had fought the British under Major General Andrew Jackson during the War of 1812. The younger Myers moved to Texas, where he fought for the Confederacy during the Civil War. Myers married Sophia Scott, then picked up again for California, arriving in 1877. He was a merchant in San Luis Rey by 1881, when he got wind that the railroad was coming.

J. Chauncey Hayes was born in 1853 and reared in the pueblo of Los Angeles. His family moved to San Diego when he was a youth. In 1875 he married Felipa Marron, who was born in San Luis Rey, and the young couple soon moved to the valley. When Hayes heard of plans for the railroad, he bought 1,240 acres in present-day South Oceanside and Carlsbad along the proposed right-of-way and the oceanfront.

The California Southern Railroad started operations in 1880. Chinese crews began track-laying the next year. By 1882 a rail link from San Diego spanned the coast to a point just north of the San Luis Rey River, where the tracks veered inland through the rugged Santa Margarita River Valley to Temecula and the Southern Pacific Railroad. Connections to San Bernardino came in 1883.

Myers moved to the site of his new town in September 1882. The next year he filed for a patent on 160 acres along the right-of-way on what was then a sheep ranch. Francis H. Whaley, later publisher of the *San Luis Rey Star* (which eventually became the *Oceanside Star*), wrote to Washington for a patent at the same time. Both claims arrived in the capital on the same day, but Myers' letter was opened first and he got the land. Myers hired 27-year-old Cave Couts, Jr., who was trained as a surveyor, to stake out the boundaries of his claim. They fell roughly between present-day 9th and Topeka streets and Hill and Pacific streets. Myers selected J. Chauncey Hayes as sole agent for land sales on the townsite, and the Hayes and Hicks Land Company was born.

There may well have been several

This is a view from the South Pacific Hotel looking southeast toward the intersection of Second (now Mission Avenue) and Cleveland streets. The train depot was Oceanside's second, and the first on the east side of the tracks. Courtesy, San Diego Historical Society-Ticor Collection

heated arguments over what to name the new town. Historian Harriet Barnard, in *Oceanside: 1769-1945,* says Myers, Hayes, and Couts got together to come up with a name to attract prospective settlers. *La Playa* ("the beach") and *Orilla del Mar* ("shore of the sea") were considered. Myers, however, insisted on an English name and he was, afer all, the owner of the townsite. Finally "Ocean Side" was settled upon.

There are also those who argue that Oceanside in a sense named itself. The early settlers of San Luis Rey and the neighboring ranchos would take off on holidays, saying "Let's go to the oceanside." So some feel the name should really be attributed to the Libbys, the Griffins, the Hubberts, the Fosses, the Marrons, the Alvarados, and the Goldbaums. Myers formalized the name when he petitioned for a post office branch in 1883.

Myers built Oceanside's first house in 1883; it was described by Samuel Tyson as "a shanty." A primitive wooden depot just a "stone's throw"

from the mouth of the San Luis Rey River was also put up at about this time. But the wet winter of 1883 and 1884 put a serious damper on Oceanside's initial growth. Stretches of the track in the Santa Margarita Valley washed out in storms. Regular runs between Los Angeles and San Diego did not become a reality until 1885 when the Surf Line between San Diego and Los Angeles opened. The greatest boon to Oceanside was that passengers traveling south from Corona through Temecula first saw the Pacific, the white sand, and the rolling breakers and smelled the sea breezes as they reached Oceanside.

With the arrival of the railroad the anticipated land boom in San Diego County and Oceanside began. In 1885 there were reports that the Atchison, Topeka, & Santa Fe Railroad had already sold 15,000 California tickets. Agents of the transcontinental roads estimated that 200,000 people would visit California that winter.

Oceanside's enterprising founders prepared themselves for the expected

The beach has long played an important role in Oceanside history. The coast had many bathhouses with the one above being the most prominent. It was located north of the present pier, near the location of the present Community Center. Built in 1885, it stood until 1904 when it was replaced by the Oceanside Electric Company's salt-water plunge. Courtesy, San Diego Historical Society-Ticor Collection

deluge. Andrew Jackson Myers built himself a $10,000 mansion in Oceanside in 1885 at present-day 3rd and Hill streets. (That structure stood until 1927.) Bathhouses were erected along the beach, and people started thinking about putting up rental cottages as well. Myers' brother, John H. Myers, built the first guest house, the Oceanside Hotel, to put up potential landbuyers. The South Pacific Hotel appeared on Pacific Street and the Tremont Hotel went up on Cleveland Street. Hawkers anxious to sell property couldn't wait for prospective buyers to arrive, but boarded trains and peddled their lots while the trains were still en route. Young pickpockets rode the same rails. Harriet Barnard described what she called Oceanside's first boom in 1886:

Trainloads of people enticed by rather over-enthusiastic advertising were hauled down from Riverside and San Bernardino on weekend excursions for wild auctions. They bought forensically described "city lots" often discovering too late that they had been staked out over muddy sloughs, thorny hills, or rocky canyons that even goats would have been unable to cross. "Some of these auctions were preposterous," said Cave Couts, Jr., in describing the period. "Buying, selling, and reselling were rampant without reason. I can remember purchasing 10 lots each a 100 feet at $25 a lot, selling them at $50, buying half of them back at $75 and selling them again for $100."

One of the primary movers in this brisk trade was J. Chauncey Hayes, undoubtedly the most enterprising, energetic, multitalented, and colorful man in the history of Oceanside.

Born in Los Angeles on June 1, 1852, Judge J. Chauncey Hayes first served Oceanside as a land agent for the city's founder, A.J. Myers. Hayes went on to serve as Justice of the Peace and City Recorder. He was also the force behind the South Oceanside Diamond, a local newspaper that began publication in March 1888. Courtesy, Oceanside Historical Society

Hayes came to San Luis Rey when he was 15 and, aside from a stint at Santa Clara College, spent the next 66 years promoting and developing north San Diego County. As sole land agent of Oceanside, Hayes sold and resold town lots time and again. And in looking at the record it appears there was little Hayes couldn't do. Over the years he acted as a banker, newspaper publisher, notary public, deputy county clerk, lawyer, bill collector, and water supplier. And he served for 20 years as justice of the peace of Oceanside.

In a sense the law was in Hayes' blood. His father, Benjamin Hayes, was one of California's most distinguished legal pioneers, having served as a federal judge for the Los Angeles and San Diego district for 10 years. The younger Hayes carried on this tradition during his two decades as justice of the peace. He dispensed the law according to the so-called "Statutes of San Luis Rey," in effect an unwritten code that he carried around in his head. As Hayes himself described it later in life:

I had the same power as a Spanish alcalde of former times. I was a law unto myself, and as we had few lawbooks, I made these statutes to fit each case in hand. You know, my statutes were absolutely perfect. There was no appeal from any decision which I made. My jurisdiciton covered the whole country roundabout here. I tried all kinds of cases. I drove all over the map, even up into the San Jacinto Valley, trying cases, and issuing legal decisions that would have astonished some of the older authorities, but which, upon examination, would have been found to contain a great deal of good medicine for offenders and healing balm for injured parties.

Hayes was no less opinionated as editor of the *South Oceanside Diamond*, which he founded in 1888. Although he was not admitted to the bar until 1890, the *Diamond* is loaded with reports of Hayes representing defendants in court. Hayes wielded considerable influence in the community, much of it through his newspaper. But Hayes' main occupation of the 1880s was building the town of

Colonel D.H. Horne's residence was located where the shopping center at Mission and Horne now stands. Horne was the president of the Wharf and San Luis Rey Flume Companies, as well as the organizer of the Bank of Oceanside. Courtesy, Oceanside Historical Society

Oceanside. He took great pride in selling the natural advantages the area offered to settlers.

Oceanside is fortunate that one of those settlers was an experienced town builder named Colonel Daniel Hussey Horne. Born in 1828 in New Hampshire, Horne is credited with being a founder and one of the primary boosters of Lawrence and Topeka, Kansas, where he lived for more than 30 years. Horne and his wife, Maria L. Hovey of Massachusetts, moved on again to Oceanside in 1885. At this time there were only a few houses, but Horne proceeded to draw on his considerable experience to help the village become a real town.

Horne built an impressive home for $8,000 at Mission and Horne streets, where the Mission Shopping Center is located today (a portion of this house was restored and moved to Division Street). Horne was the first president of the Bank of Oceanside and the town's first president of the Oceanside Board of Trustees, and he ferreted out crooked politicians as foreman of the San Diego County Grand Jury. When he died in 1894, he was buried on the grounds of his home. He is probably still there. No body was ever found or removed.

By the years 1887 and 1888 Oceanside was a boomtown incarnated. Almost overnight what had been a brushy mesa along the coast became a bustling, hustling, sprawling town. W.D. Frazee, another energetic Oceanside booster, wrote in 1888 that "within four years this place has grown from one small dwelling to a town of about 1,000 inhabitants, and the future prospect is more flattering for our rapid growth than it has ever been." Other writers promoted Oceanside as the "Mediterranean of

the West."

Service facilities jammed the streets: bakeries, livery stables, restaurants, blacksmith shops, and grocery and general merchandise stores appeared as if by magic. No less than 11 saloons slaked the thirst of a burgeoning residential population and an endless stream of transients and tourists. W.E. Crane's stage line offered daily runs to Bonsall and Mt. Fairview and other stops. It took his four-horse team four and a half hours to make the trip at a cost of a dollar and a half per person. But when the Oceanside Escondido Railway was completed in January 1888, Crane was soon out of business.

By this time the feeling around Oceanside was that its future was secure. The town was expected to be on the lines of no less than four railroads, although only three ever came to fruition. But Oceanside's greatest economic asset came not

Dr. Stroud opened this drugstore in 1888 on Second Street between Cleveland and Tremont streets. He was born in Birmingham, England, in 1856. He first located in Grand Junction, Colorado, where he was a surgeon for the Denver and Rio Grande Railroad. He eventually settled in Oceanside where he practiced as a physician and surgeon while running his drugstore. Courtesy, San Diego Historical Society-Ticor Collection

The San Luis Rey Creamery is pictured here in an image from the 1880s. Seated in the single horse wagon, just left of center, is B.F. Libby, one of the pioneer settlers of San Luis Rey who came to California in about 1867. Courtesy, Oceanside Historical Society

from the commercial ventures nor from the tourist trade, but rather from the land itself.

Oceanside's prosperity depended on a burgeoning farm population in the San Luis Rey Valley. Food crops grew readily on the fertile land, and all kinds of fruits, vegetables, and grains were able to thrive. Olives and grapes could be grown without irrigation after the first year. There was plenty of river water available, but for those who wanted to have their own supply, water could be had at 12 feet in most places. But best of all, there was now the railroad to take the farm products to market.

By mid-1888 the town had grown to the point that many people felt it should be incorporated. Frank Obear went on the record as saying, "Give me incorporation or give me death. It is the only thing that will bring life into this town." But others felt incorporation would be a liability. J. Chauncey Hayes, for example, wrote in the *South Oceanside Diamond* that a

few speculators were attempting to incorporate the town for their own private ends.

When the polls opened on June 25, 1888, Hayes formally objected to the incorporation vote. He argued that the original petition presented to the San Diego County Board of Supervisors was fraudulent and did not contain the names of 100 qualified voters. Nevertheless, the election went on as planned. In the final tally, 74 people voted for incorporation while 53 opposed it.

Hayes consulted a law firm about having the election declared illegal and printed a challenge in his paper: "Never 'Holler' Before You're Out of the Woods. And Remember 'He Who Laughs Last Laughs Best.'" Hayes may have been successful in delaying the procedure. Oceanside, however, became an official town eight days after the election, on July 3, 1888. The area incorporated covered about 1,600 acres, 10 times the size of the original townsite.

This 1892 photo captured residents
enjoying a most determined game of
tug-o-war. Courtesy, San Diego
Historical Society-Ticor Collection

CHAPTER **3**

THE
AMENITIES
OF AN
OCEANSIDE
CITY

When Oceanside was incorporated in 1888, it was a thriving farming community of 1,000 people, with a full spectrum of commercial establishments. The community was doing its utmost to attract the tourist trade, and developers and boomers were growing wealthy speculating in real estate. The railhead was carting away all the excess produce that local farmers could grow. Oceanside boosters crowed that the town was destined to become the major metropolis between Los Angeles and San Diego. With that in mind, the people of Oceanside embarked on an ambitious program to supply the amenities of city living.

By 1888 there were many homes and businesses, a few of them brick, but most of them frame structures, the timber hauled in from Palomar (then Smith) Mountain. The Bank of Oceanside building, at the corner of what is now Mission Avenue and Hill Street, was one of the most impressive structures. It housed the Huntington Drug Store, the offices of the Motor Railway Company, the Women's Christian Temperance Union, the public library, and the office of Colonel Daniel H. Horne. Cleveland

The Oceanside Pier was one of six piers constructed in Oceanside. The first was built in 1888 at Couts Street, now known as Wisconsin Street. The pier shown here was built in 1894. Located at the end of Third Street, it was Oceanside's second pier. It was known as the "iron wharf" for the four-inch iron pipe used as piling. Courtesy, San Diego Historical Society-Ticor Collection

The Bank of Oceanside was built in the winter of 1887 and stood on the north-west corner of Second and Hill streets. Colonel D.H. Horne and C.L. Morrill organized the bank with E.S. Payne as its first cashier. It was demolished in 1925 and replaced by a new building which still stands today. Courtesy, Oceanside Historical Society

Street was packed with buildings from 1st to 4th, and the sprawl was beginning to extend to 2nd (now Mission). A new depot, which also housed the trainmen, was completed in 1888. This charming gingerbread structure was remodeled in 1915 and stood until just after World War II.

The first serious thoughts of tourism as a viable industry coincided with construction of what would briefly be Oceanside's most cherished landmark. On March 22, 1887, W.H. Van Slyke, a native of the Hudson River Valley, opened the magnificent South Pacific Hotel, which cost about $50,000 to build. It was no accident that the four-story Victorian building faced the depot—it dominated Oceanside's early skyline and was the first thing seen by people debarking

from the 15 passenger trains that rolled into Oceanside each day. It offered 60 rooms and advertised a "Magnificent View of the Ocean" with "Gas, Hot, and Cold Water Piped to Every Room." The hotel was frequently touted as the "Long Branch of the Southwest."

Van Slyke built the Oceanside Opera House adjacent to the South Pacific Hotel. The two buildings went up at about the same time. The opera house was later sold to Fred Mebach. The Oceanside Silver Cornet Band, the Oceanside Orchestra, and the San Luis Rey Dramatic Society all performed there.

Van Slyke married into the Hotaling family of San Francisco, which took over ownership of the South Pacific when he died at the age of 47 in 1888. He was the victim of lung disease from his exposure to poisonous fumes during his days as a miner. Another enterprising Oceanside citizen, Melchior Pieper, rented the hotel from the Hotalings. He did extensive landscaping on the hotel grounds. A nearby field was planted with carnations and for years travelers referred to Oceanside as Carnation City. Pieper also owned a bathhouse west of the hotel on the beach. Pieper would eventually help build Oceanside's second pier at the foot of 3rd Street, right in front of his hotel.

The South Pacific was Oceanside's foremost showcase until June 13, 1896, when fire broke out on the third floor. By the time the volunteer fire department responded, the upper reaches of the building were well involved. A fire hose was hooked up to a fire plug near the opera house, but when the water was turned on the stream of water was still 25 feet short of the flames. It soon became clear that the entire structure was doomed. Pieper had virtually no insurance and Oceanside lacked a major resort-style hotel until the El San Luis Rey Hotel was built facing the ocean in 1904. It changed names twice, to the Beach Hotel, then the Colonial Inn, before it was torn down in 1966.

The South Pacific was not the only major hotel to be struck by fire in 1896. In October a blaze broke out in the Mira Mar Hotel at 3rd and Cleveland, destroying most of its upper two

The Oceanside Silver Cornet Band posed for this portrait in 1888. The band marched in parades, played on the pier, and performed in the Oceanside Opera House. The third musician from the left (standing) is James Edward Myers, son of A.J. Myers. Courtesy, Oceanside Historical Society

floors. As reported in the *Oceanside Blade,* "This is the fourth hotel to take fire this season on the coast from this point to La Jolla, and it is a strange coincidence that all the fires originated in the third story and their origin a mystery." Rumors of a firebug were rampant. The Mira Mar was repaired and reopened by Melchior Pieper.

These disasters served to remind the people of Oceanside that a reliable water supply and an organized fire fighting force were essential to prosperity and peace of mind. The problem of supplying adequate water was addressed early on. But the townspeople made much slower progress toward forming a professional fire company.

Oceanside's first water service was a wagon that brought households barrels of water. The first waterworks was established by Andrew Jackson Myers, who installed a pump by the San Luis Rey River. The 1885 *San Diego County Directory* reported, "The completion of the works, and the laying of the mains and pipes through our principal streets will be consummated in a few days, when every one will be able to drink at his own fountain." Two other water companies were owned by J. Chauncey Hayes.

In 1886 the Oceanside Water Company bought out Myers and probably Hayes, too, and by 1887 the San Luis Rey River was providing water to

Right: *The lovely gardens in front of the South Pacific Hotel were planted to entice travelers from the train depot. The hotel was located within a few hundred feet of the tracks, allowing passengers the opportunity to dine at the hotel's restaurant. Courtesy, San Diego Historical Society-Ticor Collection*

Below: *Though the South Pacific Hotel was destroyed in the 1896 fire, Oceanside's Opera House was spared. Both buildings were built by W.H. Van Slyke in 1887. The Opera House was later purchased by Frank Mebach and became the Mebach Opera House. In 1905 Mebach sold it to Melchior Pieper, the owner of the South Pacific. Courtesy, San Diego Historical Society-Ticor Collection*

bought out the Oceanside Water Company in 1890.

Soon after that, Oceanside's city trustees voted to build another 100,000-gallon water tank. In 1897 the town moved the waterworks to a five-acre parcel along the San Luis Rey River and established a reservoir near where the Rosicrucian Fellowship would spring up in 1911. Ever mindful that water was essential to attract new residents, Oceanside city trustees pumped another $45,000 into improving its water system through 1907.

By mid-1910 the city had built a water system with a capacity for domestic and irrigation purposes sufficient for a city five times its size. There were about 300 users on the metered system and they consumed about 5 million gallons of water a month. The city had its water problem well in hand.

The need for fire protection was recognized from the very beginning. Since houses were built of wood, wood and coal burning stoves were

The El San Luis Rey Hotel, built in 1904, filled Oceanside's need for a resort hotel after the South Pacific Hotel burned down in 1896. The hotel originally was to be called the "Anchorage," but "El San Luis Rey" was chosen just before the opening. It was later known as the Beach Hotel, and then as the Colonial Inn. Courtesy, Oceanside Historical Society

the townspeople. The company also inherited a 50,000-gallon wooden water tank at 3rd and Summit streets. This tank was fed by a well by the San Luis Rey River at the mouth of what is now known as Lawrence Canyon. By 1888 water was being pumped and piped for a base rate of $2.50 plus 5 cents for every 100 feet. The town

Oceanside's fire department posed in 1940 for this photograph at the "Walter Johnson" Fire Station on Third and Nevada streets. Pictured from left to right are Noel Scheunemann, Harold Davis, John Todd (sitting), Walt Johnson, Lee Jennings, Ernie Taylor, and Gus Milan (sitting on back engine). Courtesy, Oceanside Historical Society

used, and kerosene lamps were used for lighting, fire was a threat to everyone. Volunteer fire groups—the first started in 1887—were formed from time to time. But when no fires occurred the group would disintegrate, leaving the town without protection until the next volunteer fire department could be organized.

It required a disaster on the level of the South Pacific Hotel fire for Oceanside to take steps to organize an official fire fighting force. Two weeks after that 1896 blaze, Oceanside's city trustees were advised by the Water Works Committee to buy fire fighting equipment and appoint a fire marshal. Still, about 10 years later the town's only fire equipment consisted of two hose carts built by volunteers and a few wooden ladders. F.B. Schuyler was the fire marshal when another

disastrous fire hit in 1900. The flames destroyed E. Brown's dry goods store, but what really scared people was how close the fire came to consuming the whole block.

In 1906 yet another fire company was organized, and this group of volunteers formed the nucleus of a permanent fire department. Within a few years Fire Chief L.W. Stump, the owner of a grocery store, had persuaded the city to buy a 40-gallon, two-wheeled roller bearing chemical wagon, a two-wheeled roller bearing hose cart, 100 feet of two-and-a-half-inch fire hose, and 10 Sentry hand chemical extinguishers.

The automobile got into the act in 1910, when the city agreed that "a standing offer of $5.00 be made for the first team or automobile to take the chemical wagon and $3.00 for the

This unknown motorist posed proudly with his new "Tourist" horseless carriage in front of the Mission San Luis Rey. The image dates back to 1910. Courtesy, Oceanside Historical Society

first team or auto to take the hose cart to a fire in case of an alarm.'' Oceanside fire department historian John T. Wayne noted: "Lucky for the citizens of Oceanside, alarms were few as $5.00 may have been worthy of a race of machines, sending pedestrians running for protection." The first paid fire fighters were authorized by the city in 1915. They were paid 50 cents an hour, but only while they were actually fighting a fire.

The automobile quickly changed the face of Oceanside. In 1909 Hill Street was joined with a road running to Carlsbad on the south and San Clemente on the north, and sidewalks and curbs began to appear. Oceanside got another boost in 1917, when the road (later Highway 101) between Los Angeles and San Diego was paved. The new highway brought motorcars down Hill Street, as tourists explored the coast. But the greater number and greater freedom of those transiting Oceanside also brought in unwanted elements that threatened the security of the citizenry.

Oceanside enjoyed rudimentary police protection even before it became an official town. During the early 1880s there was a marshal and a few constables. The marshal kept the peace, collected taxes, and confiscated land when necessary. The town constables' main task was taking prisoners to San Diego for trial at two dollars a head. The marshal in 1888 was C.C. Wilson, and his constables included E.H. Cheever, J.K. Wilson (brother of the marshal), and J.H. Brookman. Marshal Wilson was shot and killed by a San Luis Rey cowboy in 1889 and was succeeded by E.H. Cheever.

Oceanside residents remembered the town as being especially rowdy around 1887 when the Escondido railroad was under construction. At the end of each week, Chinese, Indian, and Mexican workers roared into town. Oceanside's little jailhouse was only 20 square feet and some weekends it was standing room only. By the late 1890s there was a jail made of sheet metal on the corner of 1st and Cleveland streets. This jail was converted to a dog pound when a new concrete structure, now on display at Heritage Park, was built between 1905 and 1907. Considered very modern for the time, it consisted

Below, right: The paving of Hill Street and its integration into the larger Highway 101 resulted in an increase in tourism for Oceanside. These steam-powered rollers are shown paving Hill Street sometime around 1919. Courtesy, Oceanside Historical Society

Below, left: Horse and automobile racing were popular pastimes in Oceanside which attracted hundreds of spectators. This photo shows an automobile race along the beach in 1915. Barney Oldfield, one of the first drivers in the Indianapolis 500, raced frequently along Oceanside's beach. Courtesy, Oceanside Historical Society

of three cells, two for men and one for women.

The *Blade* of September 5, 1905, records the city's first armed robbery. The paper reported that John Manning, doorman at the Oceanside Opera House, was "waylaid by subjects unknown." The loss was $10 in quarters, and the culprits were never caught. In 1906 the city council decided to hire a special policeman, who for $50 a month patrolled the little city from sunset to sunrise. C.D. Love was Oceanside's first official policeman. Oceanside law enforcement remained primitive until 1925 when Charles Goss, town marshal since 1915, was appointed the first police chief.

Oceanside's first telephone was used primarily by the town's law enforcement officers, to keep in touch

with their counterparts in San Diego. It arrived in April 1904, and it might have come sooner had it not been for Cave Couts, Jr. As the Pacific States telephone line was making progress toward Oceanside in 1903, it met with what the *Blade* called a "rude interruption." Cave Couts, Jr., apparently didn't approve of seeing poles going across his property at Rancho Guajome. He failed to get an injunction to stop the line from going in even as telephone company crews rushed to put the wires through his property. So in the time-honored tradition of his notorious father, Cave Couts, Jr., took matters into his own hands. As the *Blade* put it, 40 telephone poles were found chopped off, "due to the perspiring efforts of Mr. Couts and his men who thereby annexed a comfortable lot of winter

Oceanside's 1936 police force consisted of (from left to right) John Martin, Fred Sickler, Norris Raymond, Harold Davis, John Todd, Warren Paxton (Chief), Guy Woodward, Ernest Taylor, and Eddie List. The police department was located in the building which currently houses Oceanside's fire department headquarters on Third and Nevada streets. Courtesy, Oceanside Historical Society

firewood, and wire."

A telephone switchboard was set up in Everetts Grocery. Called a "home phone," it was connected directly to the Santa Margarita ranch. Other independent phone systems went in, but in those days you had to have a separate phone installed for each phone company.

Telephone lines weren't the only wires going in during the early 1900s. The Pieper bath house on the beach was torn down to make a place for an electric light plant and plunge bath, according to a 1904 *Blade* report. The Oceanside Electric Company was responsible for this project. The electric plunge provided Oceanside with a warm seawater bathing area, which was enjoyed by residents and tourists alike.

The power was a great boon to Oceanside. By 1905 the Oceanside Electric Company was providing streetlights and incandescent lamps at major intersections in town. On April 22, 1905, the Oceanside Blade reported that:

The long expected "juice" is a realization in Oceanside, the plant of the Oceanside Electric Company starting up for keeps Wednesday night. The glow of the lamps was visible in all the stores and many of the residences, giving the proper metropolitan appearance. The arc street lights are ready, but the moonlit nights make them unnecessary at present. The generating plant consists of an 80-horsepower Atlas engine with a boiler. In connection will be run the apparatus for pumping and heating the salt water for the cement plunge.

These schoolchildren and their teacher posed for this picture on the steps of the Horne Street school sometime in 1910. Courtesy, Oceanside Historical Society

Oceanside's young people also enjoyed swimming in the warm plunge when they weren't occupied by more serious pursuits. Education was a serious matter to early residents of Oceanside, as well as to those who preceded them in the San Luis Rey Valley. The San Luis Rey School, founded in 1872, was situated on mission land southwest of the mission. This building was torn down in 1912 and replaced with the cement-block structure still standing today. The second schoolhouse, the Libby School, was built in the valley north of the river in 1890. Benjamin Franklin Libby was active on the school board. The Libby School was in use until 1950, when valley students started attending Oceanside schools. The Libby School building was moved to Heritage Park in 1974.

A two-story brick school was built in South Oceanside in 1886 on Cassidy Street. This school operated until 1914. By 1886 a school had also been set up in the town of Oceanside. Grammar school classes were held in a 12-by-30-foot building at 1st and Hill streets. The Horne Street School went up in 1887. It was a two-story wooden affair, offering instruction to 60 students.

Ten outlying elementary school districts were joined to form the Oceanside-Carlsbad Union High School in 1906. High school classes in algebra, Latin, history, and English were first held upstairs in the Horne Street School. In 1909 five young women made up the first graduating class, receiving their diplomas in

Theatrical productions staged by local schools were popular with both residents and merchants as well. Note the variety of advertisements above the stage. Courtesy, Oceanside Historical Society

Oceanside schoolchildren posed for this picture in 1913. The Horne Street school was located near where the present high school now stands. The school housed both elementary and high school students, with elementary-aged children on the first floor and high school students on the second floor. Since the Horne Street school contained the only secondary school in the area, it attracted students from as far south as Del Mar, and inland from Vista. Courtesy, Oceanside Historical Society

ceremonies at the Mildred Opera House, situated on the east side of Tremont Street, north of 3rd. Not until 1911 did Oceanside vote in a $15,000 bond issue for its own high school adjacent to the grammar school. Four classrooms and an auditorium were completed in 1913, and this complex, known as the West Wing, was expanded in 1920 and 1921.

Keeping the adult population informed was a task taken on by publishers in the 1880s. Among the early papers were two temperance news-papers and an anti-saloon organ. The *San Luis Rey Star* was first published in 1881 by Francis Whaley (the man who filed for the townsite at the same time as Andrew Jackson Myers). Whaley moved to Oceanside and the paper became the *Oceanside Star* in 1886. J. Chauncey Hayes' *South Oceanside Diamond* was around in the late 1880s, but stopped publication around 1891 when Oceanside got its first permanent newspaper. That paper was the *Oceanside Blade*, edited by W.S. Spencer.

Along the way, a perfunctory stab

Seen here in the production room of the Oceanside News are, from left to right, Charles Couey (Linotype operator), Charles Hart (printer) and James Welch (publisher and editor). The Oceanside News was one of many Oceanside newspapers. Others included the South Oceanside Diamond, *the* Oceanside Olive Leaf, *the* Oceanside Vidette, *the* Oceanside Herald, *the* Oceanside Star, *and the* Oceanside Blade. *Courtesy, Oceanside Historical Society*

The Oceanside Tennis Club was located near Third and Cleveland streets. Tennis, cricket, and horse racing were among the favorite activities enjoyed by Oceanside's English residents. Courtesy, Oceanside Historical Society

at establishing a public library was taken when a reading room on the second floor of the Bank of Oceanside building was so designated. When a collection of 600 books was donated to the city in 1904, the city established a public library, with Harry Brodie the first librarian at no salary. This was only one example of Harry Brodie's public-spiritedness. He also served as manager of the telegraph office, city clerk (for 27 years), assessor, and water collector.

In the late 1880s and 1890s Oceanside's residents put a lot of energy into organizing religious groups and building churches to house these congregations. In the early days makeshift quarters and shared pastors were common. But by the turn of the century local papers were advertising a diversity of church services for Baptists, Catholics, Christians, Christian Scientists, Congregationalists, Episcopalians, and Methodists. The First Methodist Church, built in 1888 and visible in all early photographs of Oceanside, is still in use at its original location. There were also two churches in the San Luis Rey Valley that bear further mention.

All Saints Church was established in the San Luis Rey Valley in 1890.

Members of this church were mainly British immigrants, who settled in the valley in the late 1880s and 1890s. Many were the families of remittance men. English custom called for the first-born son to inherit the estate, with succeeding sons getting an annual pension or remittance. Normally this was large enough to live on, so they did not have to rely strictly on farming or ranching for a living and had time to indulge in other interests.

One of these other activities was building All Saints Church and cemetery. Benjamin Franklin Libby, Alfred Morgan, Frank Reynolds, and Herbert Crouch were among the builders. The tiny English-style church could hold only about 50 or 60 people and finally closed its doors in 1925. The original building, however, still stands in the valley. There are about 200 people buried just outside the church in the little cemetery, people whose names include many of the area's original white inhabitants.

Gradually the tight-knit community in the valley disintegrated as the old settlers died, went off to fight in the Boer War, or moved into the sprawling town of Oceanside. But those who stayed added a colorful layer to Oceanside culture: their English sports of golf, tennis, cricket, horse racing and polo; their pastimes of bridge, concerts, and the theater; and their customs of high tea, socializing, and formal dressing for dinner.

The other church in the valley, of course, was the Oceanside area's first church. The Mission San Luis Rey stood neglected for 46 years until 1892, when two Franciscan friars arrived to take up residence. They were joined the next year by Father Joseph Jeremiah O'Keefe, who had dreams of restoring the mission and setting up a seminary. After some preliminary repairs the mission church was rededicated on May 12, 1893. It has served Oceanside's Catholic community and attracted visitors to the area ever since. There was, however, little these fathers could do to repair the damage done to the descendants of the original builders of the mission.

As white settlers surged into Southern California, the Luisenos lost most of their lands. Clashes between whites and Indians led to some reservations being set up at Pala, Rincon, Potrero, La Jolla, and Yapiche. Others went to nearby towns or ranches. They got some formal protection when the 1891 Act for the Relief of the Mission Indians helped them set up their own schools, courts, police force, and health care facilities. By this time there were probably less than 1,000 full-blooded Luisenos surviving. These survivors generally supported themselves by farming, ranching, or wage labor, supplemented by hunting and gathering when it was possible.

Members of the English Cricket Club gathered for this photo in 1910. The lifestyle of the English community, characterized by different sport and leisure activities, was unique to Oceanside. Courtesy, Oceanside Historical Society

Facing page: *This photo by A.C. Vroman was taken under the mission cupola facing the altar. The altar and backdrop remain more or less the same today. Courtesy, Seaver Center for Western History Research. Natural History Museum of Los Angeles County*

Right: *Born in Ireland, Father Joseph O'Keefe came to California and studied for the priesthood in San Francisco. He was ordained on September 19, 1868. His command of the Spanish language made him a valuable catalyst for the Mission San Luis Rey's restoration, a task he began in 1892. Within 20 years O'Keefe transformed the mission from a neglected ruin into a thriving and useful Catholic community. Courtesy, Seaver Center for Western History Research. Natural History Museum of Los Angeles County*

Below: *The altar at the Mission San Luis Rey, seen here in an image from 1900, was unusually flamboyant in its use of decoration. At the time of this photo, Father O'Keefe was in the process of restoring the mission. Courtesy, San Diego Historical Society, Ticor Collection*

One of the dreams of the early white inhabitants of Oceanside was to build a wharf. It was conceived not only as a way to cement Oceanside's reputation as a seaside resort, but also as a means of getting freight into Oceanside. On March 9, 1888, the *South Oceanside Diamond* reported that $28,000 in stock had been subscribed and that the wharf at present-day Wisconsin Street (then Couts Street, named for Cave Couts, Jr.) would be completed and ready for steamers by July 4. That was the day after the town was incorporated.

But progress was slow. Just 10 days before the originally scheduled opening date, the *South Oceanside Diamond* reported that the ship *Starbuck* was two miles out in the harbor and rafting the lumber in. On June 29 it reported that the lumber from the *Starbuck* was scattered three miles up and down the coast. On July 13 the word was that the completion date had been delayed until December. The wharf was plagued by problems— lawsuits, lack of funds, lack of supplies, and storm damage. People began to complain about wharf lumber being piled in the streets, obstructing traffic and causing accidents. Many of those who had

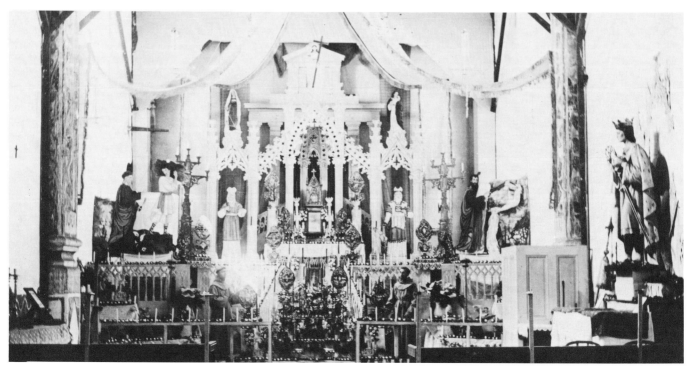

Oceanside's third pier was built in 1903. It was constructed of wood and railway steel purchased from the Santa Fe Railway Company. On the bluff to the left is the El San Luis Rey Hotel, later known as the Beach Hotel. Below the hotel is the original bath house. Courtesy, Oceanside Historical Society

pledged to buy stock did not come through with the payments. Still, by February 1889 the pier extended more than 1,200 feet out to sea.

The crusher came in January 1891, when a storm carried away all of the wharf but about 300 feet. It was quite a blow to the town. Soon afterward Melchior Pieper, the enterprising proprietor of the South Pacific Hotel, gathered up all the loose lumber and

piled it at the foot of 3rd Street. Pieper announced that the lumber would be used to build a pier in front of his hotel that would be open to the public without charge. He said that it would be 400 feet long, 12 feet wide, with 4-inch iron pipe for piling, and a 3-by-4 wooden railing to protect those who used it.

Pieper finally got financial backing from the Oceanside city fathers, who

may have delayed for fear there would be a repeat of the first fiasco. A new 400-foot iron pier at the end of 3rd Street was completed in 1894. Two years later it was extended to 600 feet. But winter storms again took a toll in 1898, and everyone realized that a more substantial structure was needed it they wanted the pier to be a permanent fixture.

A $5,000 bond issue capitalized Oceanside's third pier, completed in December 1903. This one was built of railway steel and jutted out into the ocean nearly 1,400 feet. Fishing and pleasure launches were familiar pastimes off this pier. But storms took their toll on this pier, too. By April 1915, only 800 feet would remain. But even this shortened pier was enough to help keep Oceanside afloat during one of its darkest moments.

CHAPTER **4**

~~~~~~

HARD
TIMES,
GROWTH,
AND
CHANGE

To the people of Oceanside, the flood of 1916 was more of a catastrophe than World War I, then being fought on another continent, in another world. In January of that year, 10.9 inches of rain fell on the city, 9.85 of those inches coming between the 14th and 30th of the month.

According to Mary Ronsse, who was running the local switchboard when the flood began, it all started with a rainmaker named Charlie Hatfield. Hatfield had contracted with the San Diego City Council to fill the Morena Reservoir north of Campo within a year after January 1, 1916. He was to be paid $10,000 for his services. Hatfield set up his machines, a few spindly-legged wooden frames, and ostensibly went to work.

Whether Hatfield had anything to do with it, the torrential rains that followed produced devastating flooding and property damage and the loss of 22 lives in San Diego County, including 3 in the San Luis Rey Valley. Water inundated the entire valley, from hill to hill, extending for a mile and a half and covering an area of over 1,000 acres. The first surge took out

By 1927 when the pier was constructed and the Strand paved, parades were culminating at the beach stadium. Those in attendance could enjoy speeches and dance into the night to music provided by local bands. Courtesy, San Diego Historical Society-Ticor Collection

Miraculously, the Jones Ranch was left standing after the 1916 flood. The barn at the right of the photo still stands today and is part of the Williams Ranch off Mission Avenue. Both the nearby Herman and Nelson ranches lost every building and most of their livestock. Courtesy, Oceanside Historical Society

the state highway bridge over the San Luis Rey River. Most other bridges up and down the coast were also wiped out, and Oceanside was completely isolated.

For more than a month food and supplies were dropped from boats at what was left of the Oceanside pier. The *Oceanside Blade* reported on February 5, 1916, "This week Oceanside is likewise a seaport with vessels arriving and departing, unloading and loading their cargoes, and with all the earmarks of maritime prosperity."

Charlie Hatfield took full credit for the deluge, claiming to have produced

44 inches of rain in 27 days at Morena Reservoir. But San Diego was reluctant to pay him for fear it would leave the city open to numerous lawsuits. The storm was officially declared an act of God. And the rainmaker was said to have slipped furtively out of town under an assumed name.

Plans were quickly in place to rebuild the branch of the Santa Fe railroad from Oceanside to Fallbrook. Many thousands of dollars were invested in buying supplies and paying laborers, much to the benefit of Oceanside businesses. The state highway commission paid for substantial

new bridges across the San Luis Rey and Santa Margarita rivers.

Oceanside residents were so busy building up and improving their town after the flood, they almost seem to have overlooked World War I. The article announcing the U.S. declaration of war on Germany on April 7, 1917, was only a small, almost unnoticed article on the front page of the *Oceanside Blade.* The same held true when the armistice was signed in November 1918.

Local newspapers reported a litany of accomplishments in 1917 in spite of the unfavorable climate created by the conflict. San Diego Gas and Electric Company lines in and around Oceanside were refurbished and expanded. A brick building to house the First National Bank went up on Hill Street. The public library grew by leaps and bounds in greatly improved quarters. A grinding pebble industry sprang up to provide new jobs. More

Above: *This McCallum photo shows the first train to travel over the San Luis Rey River after the flood of 1916. McCallum chronicled much of the damage caused by the catastrophic flood. Courtesy, Oceanside Historical Society*

Left: *Herbert Crouch (right) is seen crossing the San Luis Rey River after the flood of 1916. Over 10 inches of rain fell in the month of January causing flooding and property damage and claiming the lives of 22 people in San Diego County. Courtesy, Oceanside Historical Society*

On April 18, 1908, the "Great Fleet" of the U.S. Navy passed Oceanside on its historic voyage around the continent. Citizens gathered from Point Loma to San Juan Capistrano to view the naval vessels, led by the flagship Connecticut, as they made their way along the coast. Courtesy, Oceanside Historical Society

new hires were made when a $10,000 plant was put up by the Union Oil Company. The city and the state put up $30,000 to improve Hill Street. Oceanside also celebrated its first Bean Day, with some 5,000 attending, in 1917, as beans had become one of Oceanside's most profitable new crops.

Although World War I had little direct impact on the city, it did extract a human toll on some families.

Flags flew at half-mast on October 21, 1917, in honor of Oceanside's first war casualty. Young Joe McComb died of pneumonia aboard the U.S.S. *Pueblo*. McComb was not the only Oceanside son to be struck down by disease during the war. In fact, nearly half of the 112,000 American casualties in the war died of the influenza-pneumonia epidemic that swept U.S. military camps.

The influenza also reared its ugly

head in Oceanside. Dr. Robert S. Reid was quoted in the *Oceanside Blade* in November 1918 as saying, "Promiscuous visiting and assemblage must be stopped. Except where absolutely necessary, people should remain at home." The report went on to say that unless the people of Oceanside started heeding his warnings, Dr. Reid would ask the city council to force people to wear masks. Apparently this threat was never carried out.

Dr. Reid had picked up on the fine tradition of doctoring started by Dr. W.V. Nicols, who with his brother-in-law, Thomas C. Exton, managed the Exton and Nicols drugstore on 2nd Street starting in 1892. For years the doctors were forced to take horse and buggy to Fallbrook or Vista in the days of house calls. This may have inspired Dr. Reid to join forces with the Oceanside Chamber of Commerce to come up with a means to

Above: *The Oceanside pier was the site for the Bean Day Celebration in 1917. This celebration was held every year after the bean harvest and attracted residents from all around. People in attendance could sample beans cooked every way imaginable. Courtesy, Oceanside Historical Society*

Top: *This 1918 parade was held in celebration of the end of World War I. The parade originated at the new train depot and moved up Second Street. Courtesy, Oceanside Historical Society*

Above: George P. McKay and his wife, Mary Catherine Mebach, pictured here on the right, came to Oceanside in 1891. They opened their first store in 1893 on the corner of Second and Cleveland streets. In 1908 they built this store on the northeast corner of Third and Cleveland streets. The store still stands today. Courtesy, Oceanside Historical Society

Right: The Oceanside Merchants, seen here in 1910, were a prominent local baseball team. Baseball was a regular attraction until World War II, when the need for men and machines changed the nation. Courtesy, Oceanside Historical Society

improve the roads to inland areas. The idea put forward was a half-cent a gallon gas tax. This proposal went before the San Diego County Board of Supervisors, which liked the idea so much it was put up as a statewide measure. The "gas tax fund" exists to this day in California, bringing in millions of dollars for road improvements each year.

Between the end of World War I and the start of the Great Depression, Oceanside enjoyed one of its greatest periods of growth. From 1920 to 1930 the population jumped from 1,161 to 3,508, a gain of more than 200 percent. The number of square miles in the city grew from 2.6 to 8.6, an increase of more than 300 percent. This was due largely to promotional efforts and public improvements.

Tourism became big business be-tween 1920 and 1940. In 1920 Oceanside was already known as a beach resort. One of the favorite weekend pastimes was congregating on Hill Street to watch the movie stars driving from Los Angeles to Tijuana, where gambling and liquor were legal. Stores and homes popped up in addition to a number of beach cottages for the summer trade. A promenade was built along the beach so tourists could enjoy the sights without getting their shoes full of sand. The first attention was paid to the back country, and a road went in to Vista, which was expected to attract inland residents trying to escape the summer heat. It was expected that once the desert denizens experienced the pleasures of Oceanside, they would want to come back to stay.

In 1920 and 1921 the Oceanside

Thomas C. Exton and W.V. Nichols purchased this store, located at 310 Second Street (now Mission Avenue) in 1892. Nichols practiced medicine while his brother-in-law Exton ran the drugstore. They engaged in business together until Nichols' death in 1931. Both men were highly regarded, community-minded citizens who did much for the development of Oceanside. Courtesy, San Diego Historical Society-Ticor Collection

Above: Oceanside's beach was as popular in the early 1930s as it is today. Note the building beneath the pier at the far right. It was used as a community dining room for city functions. It now houses the city's lifeguard and aquatics offices. The facility at the base of the bluff, beneath the El San Luis Rey Hotel, was known as Playland. It housed a carousel (nearly obscured on the right), food booths, and carnival-type games. Courtesy, Oceanside Historical Society

Right: This photo shows Cottage City as it appeared in 1930. The view is from Sixth Street looking down Strand. Courtesy, Oceanside Historical Society

Chamber of Commerce and local boosters were doing their best to attract new residents. First off, the community sponsored a brochure to be distributed nationwide, playing up the attributes of the town. As Brian Wiersema and Mary Taschner wrote in their *The Selling of a City: Oceanside, 1920-1930:*

The Blade cooperated by running long lists of new arrivals at the city hotels, such as The Travelers on Cleveland Street. The names of persons logging in at the city tourist camps also began to appear on the front page of each edition of the newspaper. Of course, the strategy was simple if not very original. Publishing more names sold more newspapers, and many of these would be mailed back East to friends and relatives—with the names circled in ink. It's little wonder

that word of Oceanside got out efficiently and relatively quickly.

These tactics proved very fruitful for Oceanside. By the end of 1922 new building revenues had topped $150,000, a substantial sum in an era when your average home and lot could be purchased for about $2,000. Much of this business was handled by First National Bank formed by local Oceanside businessmen in 1906. It was the only bank along the coast of north San Diego County until 1926. That year the Bank of Italy, later the Bank of America, established a branch in Oceanside at Hill and Mission Avenue. Merchants began creeping from Cleveland and 2nd streets up to Hill Street to increase their visibility.

The hustle of the twenties also saw

Local horsemen posed for this portrait during a Sunday ride through Oceanside. Courtesy, Oceanside Historical Society

Although a small town, Oceanside had a love of the arts. At one time the city had an orchestra and an opera house. Pictured here in 1915 is the Oceanside Band. Though unusual at the time, the band included women members. Courtesy, Oceanside Historical Society

Oceanside get a second newspaper, the weekly *Oceanside News*, in 1921. But the town had to wait until much later in the decade to enjoy its first daily. Joe and Mark Bryan of New Mexico started publishing the *Oceanside Tribune* in 1927. The competition spurred the *Blade* to up its output to twice a week. Two years later the Beck brothers, Harold and Paul, bought both papers and consolidated them as the *Oceanside Blade-Tribune*. In 1939 the Becks also bought out the *Oceanside News*, and they continued to publish the *Blade-Tribune* until 1954, when it was sold

to Thomas W. Braden of Washington, D.C.

Oceanside's first improved subdivision was laid out east of Ditmar Street and north of Oceanside Boulevard in 1924. Plumosa Heights got its name from the *Cocos Plumosa* palms along its streets. This 12-block housing project can still be recognized from its concrete pavement and old ornamental streetlights. Deeds for the lots stipulated that sales would be to whites only. Nevertheless Plumosa Heights was in large part responsible for doubling local home construction, which went from 50 in 1923 to almost

Built by R.E. Struve, the Palomar Theatre stood on Hill Street between Third and Fourth streets. The theater provided entertainment for residents including movies, plays, and comedy routines. Note the piano and organ in front. Courtesy, Oceanside Historical Society

100 in 1924.

That year Oceanside also built its prized Palomar Theatre in the 300 block of North Hill Street. It seated 650 and the drama of the early silent movies was enhanced by a $10,000 Morton organ. This theater provided some real competition for the Elysium Theatre in the 300 block of 2nd Street.

Oceanside got some new impetus to ensure the flow of tourists to its shores in 1925, when promoters began to push a new city at San Clemente, a few miles to the north. Suddenly the citizens of Oceanside could see themselves being overshadowed. They demanded a more progressive city council to prevent them from being outstripped by the rival to the north.

It was felt that the most immediate need was for a pier. Oceanside's third pier had gotten pretty rickety because of storms between 1916 and 1924. This had left the town without the dominant feature of its claim to fame as a beach resort. Ironically the citizens of Oceanside, led by the chamber of commerce, actually defeated a $75,000 bond issue for the new pier. Their reasoning: the town wanted a $100,000 pier that could withstand the battering of wind and water, a pier that would secure Oceanside's position as a tourist resort.

The women of Oceanside, enjoying the heady new political clout offered them by the Women's Suffrage Amendment of 1920, played a key role in making this new pier a reality. Members of the Oceanside Women's Club led a campaign against two city trustees, members of the old guard led a campaign against two city trustees, members of the old guard who resisted what the newer residents called progress. A recall election failed, but the

This celebration was part of the dedication ceremony for Oceanside's fourth pier in 1927. The construction of this pier, made possible by a $100,000 voter-approved bond issue, was hotly debated. Some wanted all steel, while others decided concrete construction would be longer lasting. The compromise reached was concrete with the pier projection to consist of wood. Courtesy, Oceanside Historical Society

two trustees were ousted in regular elections in 1926. Two weeks later, on June 19, 1926, a $100,000 bond issue won by a landslide vote of 693 to 95.

Work on the pier started in January 1927. The U-shaped cement approach of this structure still stands today. The pilings were made of steel. In a celebration to end all celebrations, this 1,224-foot structure was dedicated on July 4, 1927. Three days of festivities leading up to the official opening brought between 15,000 and 20,000 visitors to Oceanside. The fireworks on July Fourth could be seen for miles up and down the coast.

This was only the start for the now fired up city council. Over the next three years streets were paved, 17 miles of new streetlights installed, and city services expanded. These activities were slowed down considerably after 1930 by the Great Depression. Still, there were developments to report. For one, in 1928 a swank settlement of exclusive homes, St. Malo, began going up in an unincorporated area south of Oceanside. By 1955 the 27-acre subdivision had been annexed to the city of Oceanside. But even to this day this restricted colony remains aloof from the outside world with a guarded gate. But it did bring in some monied, tax-paying people to help swell the city's coffers.

Outsiders also began to take an interest in the vast Santa Margarita rancho, along Oceanside's northern border. There were rumors that Al Capone had his eye on the rancho because of its miles of coastline. Those shores were reportedly a favored landing point for bootleggers during Prohibition.

In 1931 the U.S. government was making its first inquiries about Rancho Santa Margarita. Its aim at this point was to build an emergency land-

ing strip for planes flying overhead. The rancho owners were not interested in selling, but in July 1931 they did lease some land to the government at the mouth of the Santa Margarita River and an airstrip with beacon lights was established. This, of course, set the stage for the eventual takeover of the rancho by the military.

Harold B. Davis, later Oceanside's police chief, became the town's fourth officer in 1930 just as the Depression took hold. That year, a new police and fire station and courtroom was built at the intersection of Nevada and 3rd. That building remains in use to this day. At the height of the Depression Davis remembered:

The old jail on Cleveland Street was made into a "stopping off place" for transients, people passing through town

by boxcar, or by whatever other means, looking for something else to do … As a result Oceanside merchants got together and opened up a soup kitchen. It was located in the 300 block of 3rd Street, in a vacant building beneath the old Santa Fe Hotel. The local grocers donated vegetables and meat markets donated soup bones and other cuts of usable meat. Ranson's Bakery provided day-old bread and whatever else they could at the time.

On February 14, 1933, in the darkest days of the Depression, the 27-year-old First National Bank in Oceanside went under. As newspaperman Paul Beck wrote, it was a bitter Valentine's Day present that took down a number of wealthy residents. Some lost their life savings.

One man who did a lot to help Oceanside through these difficult years was John Landes, who came to Oceanside in 1922. Three years later

The First National Bank was built in December of 1925 on the northwest corner of Second and Hill streets. It replaced the ornate Bank of Oceanside building which was demolished in January of that year. This building still stands today and now houses King's Men Clothing Store. Courtesy, Oceanside Historical Society

he became city clerk, a position he held for the next 30 years. During the Great Depression, he kept the city in the black. Up until this time Oceanside city offices were housed in a variety of locations, wherever space could be found. But Landes was responsible for finding the funds to build the 3rd Street city hall building at the peak of the Depression, without the benefit of a bond issue. The city council hired construction workers at 50 cents an hour, a wage that attracted plenty at that time. In 1934 the building was completed. The total cost was under $9,000.

The Works Progress Administration (WPA) came through with help in financing two projects of importance to the city. First it helped in paving most of the streets in the area bounded by Wisconsin and 8th streets from Horne to Cleveland streets. The property owners paid for most of the material, while the federal government paid for the wages and some of the material required. In 1938—the Depression was still on—the WPA helped to construct Recreation Park on Mission west of Barnes Street. Laborers enclosed eight acres with an eight-foot adobe wall; restrooms and dressing rooms were provided inside the walls and an adobe dugout was built for softball teams.

By the end of the decade federal census figures showed Oceanside had a population of 4,651. That was a gain of just over 1,000 people. But just around the corner was a development that would shower Oceanside with national and international attention. Within 10 years the little city would be bursting at the seams and the people of Oceanside would never look back.

As hostilities in World War II escalated, the U.S. government started

looking for a West Coast training base to serve as a strategic launch pad for war in the Pacific. The military settled on the vast Rancho Santa Margarita y Las Flores. The entire parcel was bought by the U.S. Navy for $4.15 million in February 1942, a little over two months after the U.S. entered the war against Japan.

The Navy announced it intended to begin training some 20,000 marines to aid in the war effort. The land was perfectly suited for training purposes: the 18 miles of coastline offered

barracks, warehouses, dispensaries, a hospital, shop buildings—all that goes into a military post."

Incredibly, the base was ready for occupancy in just six months. The 9th Marines were in place under the command of Colonel Lemuel S. Shepherd, Jr., when the new Camp Joseph H. Pendleton was dedicated on September 25, 1942. Pendleton had been a Marine Corps hero and his widow raised Old Glory as President Franklin D. Roosevelt looked on. The heavy security throughout the camp and in Oceanside tipped off some residents that something extraordinary was occurring. A few caught a glimpse of the president as he was whisked off in his limousine to San Diego. Most Oceanside residents learned of the visit only after it was reported in the local newspapers.

An interesting sidelight to the president's visit was his interest in the old ranch house, built around 1827. There had been talk of tearing the adobe down. During his visit, however, Roosevelt requested a tour of the house and was reportedly very impressed with its historic significance. He asked California governor Culbert L. Olson to see to it that the ranch house was preserved, saying he would like to come back someday for a visit. The adobe was duly restored in 1947 with one room dubbed "The President's Room." To this day the old hacienda serves as the home of the commanding general of the base.

At its peak there were some 60,000 people stationed at Camp Pendleton. Units of the 3rd Marine Division and all of the 4th and 5th Marine Divisions got combat training at Pendleton. The camp also readied thousands of recruits to be sent to the Pacific to beef up outfits already in action. As the *Oceanside Blade-*

The Borden Building which stood on the southeast corner of Third and Tremont was occupied by the USO to accommodate and entertain the troops that poured into the new Marine Corps Base, Camp Joseph H. Pendleton. Before becoming the USO, the building housed a popular nightclub called Garrigan's. Courtesy, Oceanside Historical Society

a much-needed amphibious training site; the land stretching inland included hills, valleys, streams, and steep canyons—nearly every type of terrain needed for military exercises.

In April 1942 hordes of civilian and military construction workers descended on Rancho Santa Margarita with all the speed and purpose of a swarm of bees. The *Oceanside Blade-Tribune* reported, "Men and equipment poured in to build highways and railroad spurs; water, sewage and electrical systems;

Oceanside's fifth pier was dedicated in July 1947. At 1,900 feet it was the longest on the Pacific Coast. This pier was heavily damaged by storms during the 1970s and was finally replaced by Oceanside's sixth pier in September 1987. Courtesy, San Diego Historical Society-Ticor Collection

Tribune reported later, "Camp Pendleton became the springboard for the attack across the Pacific. It served its purpose perfectly; it might be conceded that this camp was the most important training element in winning the war in the Pacific." At 125,000 acres, it was the largest Marine base anywhere in the world until 1957, when its sister base at Twentynine Palms, a 720,000-acre facility, became an independent Marine base. To this day it remains the world's largest amphibious training base.

All this activity on Oceanside's northern doorstep had a profound impact on the city. Initially, the thousands of workers and their families who came to build the camp presented Oceanside with an unprecedented housing crunch. Restaurants and other service businesses were overflowing. Some workers who helped to build the camp moved on, but others stayed. Once the camp was open the streets of Oceanside were jammed with service personnel coming and going and the merchants rushed to provide for the daily needs of the influx. The city's official population nearly tripled in the years after 1940, reaching 12,881 in 1950.

Although the new military camp dominated the forties in Oceanside, once the war was over, the people once again took steps to shore up their hold on the tourist trade. The old steel pier, dedicated in 1927, had been damaged in a storm in 1943. But it was not until 1946 that a $175,000 bond issue was approved to rebuild the pier. Oceanside's fifth pier was completed June 1, 1947, in time for the summer tourist season. At 1,900 feet, it was then the longest pier on the Pacific Coast.

CHAPTER **5**

THE

POPULATION

WAVE

CRESTS

The first white settlement in today's Oceanside grew up around the mission, several miles from the ocean in the San Luis Rey Valley. But as soon as the town of Oceanside was founded, settlers began gravitating toward the coast, clustering in the area that is now downtown Oceanside. Many old-timers from the valley joined the wave of people moving to the bustling new town, a pattern of movement that would persist for decades. But in recent years, under the pressures of progress, that trend has reversed itself. As a result, people, homes, and businesses have been rolling back east across El Camino Real, the ebb and flow of the city's growth mirroring the breakers advancing and receding on Oceanside's beach.

The city of Oceanside had started to inch eastward between 1920 and 1940. But in 1949 the city launched an aggressive campaign that would see the completion of 34 annexations within five years. Carlsbad voters put a squelch on any plans of moving south, voting to keep their own identity in 1952. At this point Oceanside still only covered about nine square miles. But during the sixties, seventies, and eighties, the city grew through annexations to its present 40.7 square miles. In this same period

Located on Hill Street, Huckaby's Department Store was built in 1912 as J.E. Jones Hardware Store. On the left is the old First National Bank building. It is shown here in 1947 as a National 5-10-25 Store. Courtesy, Seaver Center for Western History Research, Natural History Museum of Los Angeles County

To meet the need for housing, O.U. Miracle introduced Miracle Village. Located in South Oceanside, the development offered 1/4-acre homesites to incoming residents. Most of the homes still stand today in what continues to be a highly desirable neighborhood. Courtesy, Oceanside Historical Society

of time Oceanside's population rose phenomenally from 12,881 in 1950 to 102,863 in 1987. Most of this growth was due not to tourism, but rather to continued expansion at Camp Pendleton and the acquisition of a number of new industries.

Following World War II there was a lull in activity at Camp Pendleton, though it would prove to be short-lived. The tent camps went up again with the outbreak of hostilities in the Korean War. The 1st Provisional Brigade sailed from Camp Pendleton for Korea on July 15, 1950. By 1953 the camp was known as "The Gateway to Korea." Nearly 200,000 marines passed through the camp on their way to the Far East.

This activity did much to help Oceanside along economically in the fifties. By the end of the decade the camp had a monthly payroll of $4 million. Undoubtedly Pendleton marines dropped some of that cash in Oceanside business and entertainment establishments. And a good number of marines, navy personnel with families, and civilian camp workers set up housekeeping in Oceanside as well. From 1946 to 1952 the value of housing starts leaped from $1.5 million to more than $6 million a year. Between 1950 and 1960, the population of Oceanside nearly doubled to just shy of 25,000.

Much of the profits from the postwar boom were pumped back into the community. Congestion on Hill Street had become a problem and construction of the Carlsbad-Oceanside Freeway, eventually a part

In November 1953 a ribbon-cutting ceremony was held celebrating the opening on I-5 from Buena Vista to Brooks Street near Oceanside. Courtesy, Oceanside Historical Society

of Interstate 5, began in March 1951. Its 10.7 miles cost $9.5 million to build. Sales tax money was used to build the Oceanside Community Center in 1956. This $134,000 stucco and concrete building became a magnet for community activities, with a virtually continuous schedule of lectures, concerts, meetings, and sporting activities.

Local schools were hard-pressed to keep up with the growing demand for classroom space. By 1953 nearly 2,500 children were enrolled in the six elementary schools in the Oceanside-Libby Union School District. One year later the new Mission Road School was completed and new expansions were planned in existing schools. The Oceanside-Carlsbad Union High School had 700 students. The town of Carlsbad, however, in keeping with its desire to maintain autonomy, withdrew from that school district in 1958 and started its own. That eased crowding in Oceanside schools for a while.

The demand for higher education had been met from 1934 to 1964 by the Oceanside-Carlsbad Junior College, which held classes at the high school. By 1960 there were 300 students at this junior college, and they were getting crowded out by the once-again swelling high school enrollment. Oceanside voters came to the rescue with a $3.5-million bond issue. MiraCosta College was dedicated in southeast Oceanside in May 1965.

Two new phenomena appeared on

Bushy Graham, seen here in 1940, owned several Oceanside eateries including the popular Graham Drive-ins located on both North and South Hill streets. Courtesy, Oceanside Historical Society

Oceanside's landscape as the tumultuous sixties and seventies advanced. The first modest shopping centers began to pop up in Oceanside as suburban living became the catchword of the day. Plans were developed for a regional super mall in the sixties. The Plaza Camino Real was situated just beyond the Oceanside city limit in Carlsbad in 1969. All through the seventies, Oceanside grew at three times the county average and other shopping centers sprouted in Oceanside to keep up with a growing population base.

The other phenomenon that would change the face of the growing city was the arrival of the industrial park. Oceanside acquired its first electronics company in the 1950s with the arrival of the Vacuum Tube Products Company, started in the garage of Harold Ulmer. In 1958 he built a plant at East Short Street (now Oceanside Boulevard) and Canyon Drive. That year the Triplett Electrical Instrument Corporation of Ohio built the first plant in the Oceanside Industrial Center, east of town on Highway 76 in the San Luis Rey Valley. Electronics firms were exactly the type of clean, light industry that the people of Oceanside most wanted to attract. And the businesses seemed only too happy to come.

Oceanside Municipal Airport was in the planning stages in 1958, just as industry began to appear. It was designed to handle private and light commercial air traffic. In 1962 it was strategically located close to Highway 76 between Interstate 5 and Highway 395 (now Highway 15). By the late 1980s it would be within minutes of nearly a dozen Oceanside industrial parks.

Ever conscious of its image as a tourist resort, the city of Oceanside

put tight restrictions on these industrial parks. They had to be low-rise and set back from the streets, with adequate parking and off-road space for loading and unloading trucks. Beautification efforts and anti-litter drives brought Oceanside national

and state recognition in the mid-seventies. Oceanside was named California's cleanest city in 1975. And the freeway interchange at Interstate 5 and Highway 78 won a national beautification contest for Outstanding Example of Landscape Treatment Along Roadsides and Interchanges in 1976.

International events again would have an impact on Oceanside in the Vietnam era. The first U.S. military advisers were sent to train the South Vietnamese army in February 1955.

By the early sixties Americans were going overseas in large numbers. At the peak of the war in 1967, nearly half a million men and women were stationed in Vietnam, and the city next to Camp Pendleton was booming again. Payroll during the Vietnam War peaked at $133 million, including civilian workers. By 1970 Oceanside's population had broken 40,000.

President Lyndon B. Johnson made an appearance at Camp Pendleton in November 1967. The occasion was the 192nd anniversary of the U.S. Marine Corps. Some 15,000 marines and their families turned out to welcome the president. The visit was not without political overtones. Johnson told the crowd, "The road we travel in Vietnam to an honorable peace is not an easy road." He concluded his appearance with a visit to men wounded in the Vietnam War at the camp's U.S. Naval Hospital.

Even as Oceanside enjoyed the benefits of its proximity to Camp Pendleton, the relationship left Oceanside with one frustrating legacy. Federal funds had financed a 1,400-foot jetty in 1942 to protect the moorings at Camp Pendleton boat basin. Unfortunately, this jetty interrupted the normal flow of sand along Oceanside's beach—the jetty allowed the sand to drift away from but not back to shore. The erosion on Oceanside's beach was evident almost immediately, and it contributed to a real problem for the city that would take years to repair.

The federal government, however, refused to admit the erosion was caused by its jetties until 1953. Sand from dredging at the military harbor was used for a time to replenish Oceanside's beach south of the pier, where erosion was taking its toll.

A potential remedy came along in 1962 and 1963, when the federal government helped finance a small-boat harbor for Oceanside, adjacent to the Camp Pendleton boat basin. Millions of cubic yards of sand were returned to the Oceanside beach in preparation for the building of the Oceanside Small Craft Harbor. Millions of dollars would come into the local economy as support businesses began popping up, everything from lodging, restaurants, and gift shops to boatyards, sporting goods stores, and fishing-supply stores. Thanks to the efforts of Oceanside mayor Irwin Sklar, the new boat basin was dedicated in June 1963 amid much fanfare. And when the nearby Waterside Cape Cod Village was completed, the harbor area became a major tourist asset for Oceanside.

On the other hand the harbor did little to correct the erosion that was tearing away at Oceanside's prime tourist attraction. In 1967 the federal government finally took full responsibility and ordered engineers to come up with a permanent solution. The city dumped tons more sand on the beach between 1965 and 1981, most of it coming from dredging operations in the civilian harbor. Beach nourishing programs in the 1980s, for the most part paid for by the government, did much to rectify the problem. An experimental sand bypass solution was in the works in the late 1980s.

The other major challenge facing Oceanside was the decline of its downtown. The downtown area had been suffering ever since Oceanside began its march up to the east. Businesses headed for the suburbs to keep up with population growth there. As it happened in many cities nationwide, when the tax base downtown lost ground, necessary services and

*The ocean blue colors of the city flag
wave proudly over the Oceanside pier.
Since its incorporation Oceanside has
established itself as a progressive city
without losing its charm as a seaside
community. Photo by Michele Burgess*

The orange glow of a setting sun surrounds the Oceanside pier in this beautiful twilight image. Photo by Joseph M. Daley

Below and right: *The Cape Cod Village by the harbor, with its specialty shops and fine restaurants, offers a beautiful setting for visiting tourists and sailors alike. Photos by Michele Burgess*

This popular pleasure harbor, built in 1963, can accommodate over 800 boats and is still expanding. The harbor attracts weekend sailors from the entire California coast. Photo by Michele Burgess

No longer a haven for crime, Oceanside's revitalized downtown district stands as a model for progress amongst comparable cities. Photo by Chris Bryant

Left: *Established in the 1940s Camp Pendleton today represents the world's largest amphibious training base. Photo by Michele Burgess*

Below: *Oceanside's new transit center features both train and bus transportation in the most modern complex of its type in the state. Photo by Michele Burgess*

A warm sunset settles peacefully over Oceanside's pleasure harbor. Photo by Michele Burgess

Above: *Services are still held in the beautifully restored and maintained chapel of the Mission San Luis Rey. Photo by Reed Kaestner. Courtesy, Zephyr Pictures*

Left: *The Heritage Park Village and Museum, dedicated to the future on July 4, 1976, reflects on more than 100 years of Oceanside history. Visitors can stroll through old buildings equipped and furnished as they may have been in the 1800s. Photo by Michele Burgess*

Facing page: *This photo, in sharp contrast to early Mission pictures, illustrates the growth and beauty that characterize the San Luis Rey Valley. The nearly 200-year-old Mission is a constant reminder of Oceanside's rich heritage. Photo by Stephen Whalen. Courtesy, Zephyr Pictures*

Above: *Surfing is a regular pastime for many Oceanside residents. Photo by Patricia Hoffman*

Right: *This couple is enjoying a peaceful day of fishing off Oceanside's pier. Photo by Patricia Hoffman*

The winner of the 1986 Oceanside Horny Toad Triterium crosses the finish line at the South Strand. Oceanside has the perfect conditions for staging this contest which consists of a rough water swim, bicycling, and running. Courtesy, Rob Beck

These beach cottages, though over 50 years old, retain the picturesque view of Oceanside's past. Built originally as the Surf Motor Court, and now known as Robert's Cottages, these distinct vacation homes are familiar landmarks to vessels passing along the coast. Photo by Stephen Whalen. Courtesy, Zephyr Pictures

improvements were neglected. The district, in short, had become a drain on the whole town. This decay and deterioration contributed to one of Oceanside's most difficult moments.

As the Vietnam War wound down in the early seventies, there were more than 40,000 marines stationed at Camp Pendleton, many of whom would never see action in what had become a highly controversial war. On weekends hundreds of soldiers would head off-base for some civilian rest and relaxation. The nearest city was Oceanside and many marines congregated downtown, where a collection of rather unsavory establishments had moved in to replace the legitimate ones moving inland. Discipline broke down to such an extent that Harold Keen, a San Diego newspaperman wrote: "From the July 4, 1973, downtown riot—which brought in swarms of deputies, California Highway Patrolmen and Carlsbad police to help Oceanside cops subdue hundreds of belligerent marines and civilians—to the traumatic summer of 1975, when crime reached a frightening crescendo, Oceanside suffered an identity crisis."

The marines weren't the only rowdy element in Oceanside. The city's location on the main freeway made it a popular stop for revelers traveling between Los Angeles and San Diego. And the rapid growth Oceanside had experienced taxed the ability of Oceanside's modest police force to maintain the upper hand. These elements converged on Oceanside all at once against a backdrop of civil dissent and national distress over the upheaval in federal government stemming from Watergate.

The crisis deeply disturbed the people of Oceanside. Starting in 1975 city government took the lead in get-

ting the city back on course. Mayor Howard Richardson made some personnel changes at city hall, installing veteran Oceanside police officer Rolf Henze as chief of police and Dan Stone, formerly city manager of Riverside, as Oceanside's city manager. The final member of this new law-and-order troika came on board in 1976 after Howard Richardson decided to return to private life. Paul Graham, the newly retired commanding general at Camp Pendleton, was elected mayor of Oceanside. Graham was thoroughly familiar with Oceanside's crime problems and the role the marines played in them. In late 1976 Graham, Henze, and Stone launched a concerted campaign to clean up and revitalize the city's downtown.

Police Chief Henze began by shifting officers from traffic duty to a special anti-crime force to clean up the troubled downtown zone. His force was augmented through an almost unprecedented arrangement with the Marine Corps, which permitted the city to employ off-duty non-commissioned officers to help keep the peace. Most trainees would think twice before starting trouble with a noncom who would have complete control of him come Monday morning. The new city leaders also spearheaded the effort to ban drinking on public streets and beaches. It all created a dramatic turnaround for Oceanside. The crime rate, which had risen 35 percent in 1973 and nearly 15 percent in 1975, actually dropped by about 4 percent in 1976. With the exception of one or two years, criminal activity decreased steadily into the next decade, and in the late 1980s the Oceanside crime rate was below that of most other comparable cities.

Much of that progress can be

Facing page: The sun setting over the Pacific silhouettes the Oceanside pier. Photo by Mark E. Gibson

attributed to the redevelopment drive that began officially in 1975. The Oceanside City Council was given the added task of serving as the Community Development Commission. The commission came up with a plan that outlined redevelopment in broad strokes. Among the goals were revitalizing downtown, eliminating urban blight, promoting quality development, increasing the tax base, creating more jobs, and developing a pleasing environment to attract people back to downtown. Although the objectives were couched in general terms, they gave the redevelopment commission wide latitude in the projects it could undertake, projects that would drastically change the face of downtown Oceanside over the next decade and a half.

Even before the redevelopment program was finalized, a new housing project was completed on Hill Street at the north end of the city, only 550 feet from the beach. The project, known as Sea Village, was the first residential community to be built in the downtown area for more than a decade. The success of the Sea Village experiment encouraged developers to take on another housing project, this one with the blessing of the redevelopment commission.

In 1986 ground was broken for an ambitious condominium complex right on the Strand at 6th Street. The 243-unit luxury complex known as San Miguel was to be built in four stages, and the Mediterranean-style condos in the first stage sold even before construction was completed. In addition to amenities like fireplaces, tiled wet bars, and security guards and gates, San Miguel offered a private recreation area with spectacular ocean and harbor views.

Other developers with big ideas,

however, got a clear message from Oceanside voters in 1987. That was the year Oceanside approved Proposition A, a slow-growth mandate. The new law put a cap on new residential construction, though it exempted industrial, commercial, and redevelopment projects. It was the strongest indication yet that the people of Oceanside were concerned about their quality of life being eclipsed by overdevelopment.

Oceanside opened up more prime downtown space when the city's bus and train stations were consolidated into one complex. The spacious new transit center was completed in January 1983. The 25,000-square-foot depot was open on four sides for security purposes, but roofed over to protect travelers from the weather. There were separate ticket offices for trains and buses, although they could now load and unload side by side. The depot had a good, clean fast-food restaurant, plenty of benches, and well-tended washroom facilities, altogether a favorable introduction for travelers to the city.

Another transportation headache was eliminated in the late 1980s when the railroad switching yard along the main line between Missouri Avenue and 7th Street was relocated. The old site on Mission Avenue, two blocks east of the waterfront, was on a direct route from mid-city to the ocean. As many as 99 times a day it was blocked by the time-consuming switching maneuvers, causing aggravating delays for visitors and residents alike. The relocation of the switching yard to the southeast corner of Camp Pendleton was the culmination of 10 years' work. Direct access to the Pacific Ocean was now possible along a palm-lined Mission Avenue, which was scheduled to be extended to Pacific Street. The city of Oceanside threw a big party in January 1988 to celebrate removal of the switching yard. But the real bonus was the 20 acres of downtown that were freed up to provide a mixture of retail stores, office space, and multifamily residential space—in other words, tax-producing land.

The beach itself also underwent improvements. The streets, the beachfront, the community center, the amphitheater, and the parks were all being refurbished. A Strand Beach Park of 2.2 acres was to feature a "tot lot" for children, public restrooms, a gazebo, and other recreational facilities. Another park and view area was the Pacific Street Linear Park between Wisconsin and 1st Street. A half-million-dollar expansion extended it four blocks from 1st to 5th streets on the west side of Pacific Street.

By far the most ambitious redevel-

opment project, however, was the new civic center. It was expected to occupy three blocks of the 375 acres in the redevelopment zone. Previously, anyone conducting business with the city might have to visit several offices in various buildings. Slated to go into the main project were all of the city's administrative offices, harbor offices, firehouse, a main library double the size of the old one, and a $3.5-million, three-story retail and office building, which would yield additional income to the city. Mainly through the efforts of the Oceanside Historic Preservation Advisory Commission, the old city hall and fire station were included in the civic center plans in 1987. One sacrifice in the name of progress had to be made. The old Palomar Theatre was torn down to make way for the new complex. Groundbreaking for the project took place in March 1988.

The intensity and rapid progress of

Irving Gill, noted architect, designed and built several buildings in Oceanside. Shown here is a rendering of the proposed civic center in 1929. Although he designed the entire civic center, only the fire station at Third and Nevada streets and City Hall were ever completed. Courtesy, San Diego Historical Society-Ticor Collection

redevelopment attests to Oceanside's faith in its future. And the fact that the citizens of Oceanside built Heritage Park attests to their fierce pride in their origins. Still, it wasn't until the 1980s that an official historic preservation group was organized. The Oceanside Historic Preservation Advisory Commission was formed in 1983 and one of its first projects was designing a historic district around the mission. It was projected to be a complex somewhat like San Diego's Old Town with a resort hotel and shopping village at the intersection of Mission Avenue and Peyri Drive. Tight guidelines were to limit the height of these buildings to preserve the view of the mission in the valley. A group of citizens formed the Oceanside Historical Society in 1985. Its avowed purpose was to preserve artifacts, memorabilia, books, maps, journals, photos, and manuscripts pertinent to Oceanside's past. In addition, it meant to work with the city and private property owners to identify and save significant buildings.

Both historical groups helped in planning Oceanside's centennial celebration in 1988. A Fourth of July festival attracted thousands to a series of concerts, pageants, and fireworks. But the real centerpiece of the festivities was the new pier, renovated and reopened in September 1987. Oceanside's 1946 pier had fallen victim to angry seas and was condemned in 1983. The new 1,600-foot pier cost $5 million to build. This pier played an unusual role in helping Oceanside celebrate its 100th birthday. Promoters of the centennial festivities came up with an idea to help finance the celebration. For $25, subscribers could have a name carved into the wood along the rails. Thousands of past and present Oceanside residents

jumped at the chance to own their own little piece of this symbol of Oceanside's past.

The future for Oceanside looks bright in 1988. There are hopes of turning the harbor and beach into a mini-convention mecca with the addition of a major hotel and convention center. And despite the collective focus on the city's visible downtown and beach areas, many residents in reality are turning their eyes inland. For the first time in Oceanside history, most of the popu-lation is living east of El Camino Real. And most growth in population and industry is expected to perpetuate that trend. Camp Pendleton remains an economic anchor in the late eighties, but it is no longer the city's only claim to prosperity. Oceanside's centennial seems to mark the beginning of a new era for the city. Oceanside is no longer perceived as an adjunct to Camp Pendleton; in fact, the tide is beginning to go the other way.

Facing page: *Oceanside's pleasure harbor can accommodate over 800 boats. Photo by Michele Burgess*

Below: *Known popularly as "the cannon," this gun was once a familiar fixture in Oceanside. Courtesy, Oceanside Historical Society*

CHAPTER **6**

103

PARTNERS IN PROGRESS

The year was 1887. California had been a state for only five years when a newly published book on San Diego County mentioned the village of Oceanside—population 1,000—where, two years earlier, the railroad had arrived. Douglas Gunn, in his July 1, 1887 analysis of San Diego County cities, wrote that "A town less than two years old [Oceanside] ... is undoubtedly destined to be the largest and most important town in the county, outside of San Diego."

Gunn's words were decidedly prophetic. Oceanside, which was incorporated as a city on July 3, 1888, precisely a year after the book was published, is today just about what Gunn said it would be: probably the largest and most important suburban city in the county.

The coming of that railroad connecting San Diego and Los Angeles brought new settlers to Oceanside, with concomitant needs for housing, food, clothing, and transportation, all of which forged the beginnings of a major North County economic force, a community. Soon there was a railroad inland to Escondido, and Oceanside became a north-south, east-west rail switching and fueling center.

The new settlers were bold and entrepreneurial. Businesses sprang up alongside the railroad tracks, and a new downtown boomed.

It wasn't until World War II, how-ever, that major changes occurred. With the creation of Camp Pendleton in 1942—one of the largest military bases in the world—Oceanside began to boom.

With the city's biggest payroll the Marine Corps immediately became Oceanside's largest employer, and the one where most of the area's jobs originated, both civilian and military.

People and industry have flocked to Oceanside from both Orange and San Diego counties since the late 1960s, raising the city's population to well in excess of 100,000.

By the turn of the century the city's population is expected to grow by at least half its present number, largely because Oceanside is a community in the old-fashioned sense—an aggregate of people and businesses with a sense of togetherness and a spirit of oneness.

The people, establishments, and organizations whose histories are related on the following pages embody that spirit. They also recognize their commitment to the community and its needs, giving the support that contributes to the solidarity of Oceanside. They have chosen to support this important literary chronicle of the city they have helped to nurture—and continue to strengthen.

The prophetic Douglas Gunn—who based his now 100-year-old predictions for Oceanside largely on the basis of the arrival of the railroad—would be pleased that the railroad is alive again, with commuter trains arriving and departing at a regional transportation center in downtown Oceanside. The old switching yards, however, have been moved northward to make room for downtown redevelopment, which promises to create a bright new center of interest for the city.

J.E. Jones proudly displays the goods for sale in his hardware store in 1908. During 1912 he began construction of a new store on the southeast corner of Second and Hill streets. The building was later known as Huckaby's and is still there today. Courtesy, Oceanside Historical Society

OCEANSIDE HISTORICAL SOCIETY

A philosopher once wrote, "Those who ignore history are condemned to repeat it."

As Oceanside begins its second century as a city, a group of its forward-looking citizens believes a look back in time will help shape its future. With thoughts such as these of paramount concern to the founding members of the Oceanside Historical Society, a few motivated residents have set forth to document this city's history.

The society was founded in 1985 by a handful of people anxious to find a way of properly preserving the past for future generations. Today the 100-member society is recognized by the city as a credible historic screening organization for area development. And with plans for a museum in which to display the city's valuable artifacts, the foundation has set up a photo archives to store documents of historical significance.

Its first task was to compile an index of books, pamphlets, letters, and other printed material that had been written about Oceanside through the years, with the goal of acquiring them as the nucleus of the history section of a public library—ultimately, a museum research library. A secondary but equally significant goal was to create an intimate oral and video history through interviews with early residents of the community to preserve their recollections of life in Oceanside.

"We found there is a certain urgency to our cause as we watch buildings come down, traditions change and evolve, and memories fade," explains a charter member, commenting on the fast-growing and changing North County area. "It would be overly dramatic to say that time is running out; but the clock is certainly ticking."

The fledgling society has gained stature, credibility, and community acceptance as a result of its careful research, particularly in its documentation of and reliance upon factual material. Oceanside residents now seem to treat historic sites with more

Built in 1887, the Bank of Oceanside building has played host to a variety of occupants, from church gatherings and the board of trustees to dentists' offices and the library. Photo circa 1907

respect. This is an apparent outgrowth of the society's work with the City of Oceanside, which periodically asks for comment on the impact of new developments on areas of historic significance.

In planning downtown redevelopment, several city council members have considered the possibility that the city's main fire station at Third and Nevada may become available to the historical society for use as a headquarters and museum. The landmark structure, designed by noted architect Irving Gill, is to be vacated when a new fire head-

quarters is constructed.

The publication of this book represents the most important aspect of the Oceanside Historical Society's work to date. The photos included provide a rare glimpse into a time most of us can only read about. Through them can be seen the determination and foresight of the imaginative few who have made this city such a desirable place to live, work, raise families, and vacation.

This book would not have been possible without the help of so many who gave unselfishly of their time, research talents, and family memorabilia.

Oceanside residents gather at the pier to watch the passing of the Great Fleet in 1908. The pier shown was Oceanside's third and was built in 1903.

MIRACOSTA COLLEGE

MiraCosta College, which serves the north coastal area of San Diego County, is one of California's many widely acclaimed, tax-supported, two-year community colleges.

For more than a half-century it has offered coastal residents from Oceanside to Del Mar a wide variety of comprehensive educational opportunities. Students may obtain immediate job skills or complete an associate degree in preparation for a bachelor's degree.

Operating under state law and directed by a seven-member board of trustees, MiraCosta College currently serves about 10,000 students from its two campuses—the main facility in Oceanside and the new 44-acre San Elijo satellite campus in Cardiff. "We view ourselves as a community center for lifelong learning," says Dr. H. Deon Holt, president. "We act as a cultural focal point for the region in terms of theater, music, and art."

MiraCosta provides an associate degree, prepares students for the final two years in the state's four-year college and university systems, and offers specialized vocational education and life-enriching community education classes. One of its primary missions is to assist the overall educational structure by assessing students' skills and abilities and providing necessary counseling, tutoring, financial aid, and job placement.

One of the college's important goals is to provide basic skills education for students who have an inadequate academic background for regular college work. One of the most popular programs in this area is English as a second language.

MiraCosta got its start as Oceanside-Carlsbad Junior College in 1934 on the grounds of Oceanside High School. It was the height of the Depression; because of widespread unemployment, the community decided that high school graduates should be given an opportunity to go on to college where they could work toward a bachelor's degree or learn a vocational skill.

The mission has not changed, but it has been expanded to include education for students of any age who want

An aerial view of MiraCosta College's 121-acre hilltop campus.

MiraCosta College serves 10,000 students yearly, offering university transfer courses and a variety of vocational programs.

to improve the quality of their lives, for whatever reason.

Keeping construction of college facilities apace with area growth has always been a challenge, both economically and in terms of timeliness. In the mid-1960s the campus was relocated to a 121-acre hilltop site just west of College Boulevard at One Barnard Drive, which is expected to accommodate growth for several decades to come.

To emphasize its regional nature, the name MiraCosta was adopted by the trustees in 1965, and the two-city designation of Oceanside-Carlsbad was dropped. "MiraCosta" is derived from a Spanish term meaning "behold the coast," and refers to the Oceanside campus' picturesque hilltop setting with a panoramic view of the Pacific Ocean and coastal mountain range.

Operating policies at the college have always been set by local trustees, and the MiraCosta governing board has been a relatively stable and harmonious one. A major problem has been in keeping the fast-growing region aware of the college and its community-centered academic offerings.

Says Holt, "We believe that as the area grows in population and the tax base expands, MiraCosta College will be able to continue broadening the curriculum and enhance its ability to meet community needs."

THE LIGHTFOOT PLANNING GROUP

For 15 years Lou Lightfoot has helped shape the city of Oceanside. As a planner—first in city government and then with his own consulting group—he has been instrumental in developing most of the city's major residential areas, commercial centers, and the creation of a major industrial area in central Oceanside that now constitutes the economic backbone of the community.

The city doubled in size while he and his associates worked with government, entrepreneurs, developers, and environmentalists for a better understanding of community planning and its underpinnings in citizen involvement, community needs, market demands, political concerns, and aesthetics.

"We helped guide these projects into being while preserving and enhancing the city's quality of life," Lightfoot says. "Our philosophy of maintaining a sense of neighborhood and protecting the environment while meeting public needs, we believe, has

helped create a new community within the context of Oceanside's existing values."

He and his staff have been involved in almost every major project undertaken in Oceanside in the past decade, outlining needs and drafting plans for such things as streets, parks, schools, and sewer and water facilities, as well as mapping strategic areawide plans for future projects.

Louis N. Lightfoot, president of the Lightfoot Planning Group, started the firm in 1978 when he left the city of Oceanside after five years' service in the planning department, the last three as planning director. "I began by subletting a small office from one of my clients; it was so small we referred to it as a broom closet," recalls Lightfoot.

The Lightfoot Planning Group's 18 planners and landscape architects are recognized as a major planning force in the Oceanside area. Lou Lightfoot (below) stands in front of the firm's new building. At right is the firm's first building.

Today his land-use planning firm owns and occupies two buildings across from the new civic center, which Lightfoot recommended be built as part of a long-range downtown redevelopment study completed while he was planning director.

Lightfoot's 18 planners and landscape architects are recognized as a major planning force in Oceanside and constitute one of the leading land-use planning firms in the county. The firm has done planning or consulting in every political jurisdiction in San Diego County and enjoys a growing reputation throughout the rest of Southern California. Its client list includes many of the major commercial and residential developers in Southern California.

North San Diego County, particularly the Oceanside area, has been in the midst of a building boom the past decade as counties reach out for room to grow. As a city planner Lightfoot established the groundwork for the city's subsequent growth management strategy. Since then his firm has been an influential force in implementing that municipal strategy by encouraging clients to not only "live by city rules" but to support them.

"In giving advice on project feasibility, design, and implementation," says Lightfoot, "the company follows strong internal guidelines that call for a sensitivity to the community as well as to political and economic factors."

BEST WESTERN MARTY'S VALLEY INN

In 1946 a young Army captain and his wife visited Oceanside as part of a trip up and down the West Coast, seeking the "right" community in which to start a business, build a home, and raise a family.

They decided that Oceanside—then a small town of about 9,000, all adjusting to the end of World War II—was exactly the type of community they wanted. It was friendly, the people were warm, the schools were good, and it offered a close-knit downtown with opportunities for an entrepreneur.

"Marty" Schroder and his wife, Edith, bought a small coffee shop at 407 Mission Avenue for $3,500 and began to put down roots. Four decades later any Oceanside resident who doesn't know Marty, his wife, and their two sons is a newcomer. The Schroders and their sons, Jim and Ron, are widely recognized as pillars of the business community and are involved in hotel management, civic, and social activities.

Over the years the family operated a series of restaurants, each one larger than its predecessor, until they began to "grow" a hotel on the site of one of their biggest enterprises, Marty's Valley Inn, North County's first big dinner house with both dancing and entertainment.

Today they operate Best Western Marty's Valley Inn at 3240 Mission Avenue. A 111-room hotel and 225-seat conference center, it is the largest complete full-service facility in the city.

Marty operated his second restaurant, Marty's Steak House, at 206 North Hill Street for many years, selling it in 1964 in order to concentrate his management skills on the new inn venture on Mission Avenue. In 1954 he purchased 10 acres of land as an investment "way out in the boonies" on Mission Avenue and opened Marty's Valley Inn a year later, thereby operating two restaurants.

"Mom kept books, Dad ran the restaurants, and we kids washed dishes, swept, waited on tables, and did any-

thing else that needed doing," recalls Jim, who today manages the enterprise. Ron, successful in real estate, retains his economic and management interest in the family business.

The Schroder family's hotel is the centerpiece of their holdings, which include ownership of nearby buildings occupied by an auto parts store and a service station. The restaurant aspect of Marty's Valley Inn, adjacent to the ho-

Ground was broken for Best Western Marty's Valley Inn in 1960. In the center are Marty and Edith Schroder. Also present are several civic leaders of the era.

The Schroder family (left to right): Marty, Ron, Edith, and Jim.

tel, was sold a few years ago and today is known as The Grove.

More than 42 years of business transactions have given the Schroders a reputation for fairness and an abiding interest in returning some of their good fortune through community endeavors.

Marty was president of the California Motel Association, charter president of the San Luis Rey Shrine Club, a member of the Oceanside Rotary Club and chamber of commerce, and—of particular interest for him—the armed forces YMCA, for which he has raised much money toward improving relations between the community and the military. Edith has been active in the Soroptimist Club for many years.

Jim has followed in his father's footsteps in specific civic endeavors but has a particular interest in the community at large, which he praises for its hospitality, friendliness, and willingness to help others. Fluent in Spanish, he is also a supporter of cultural exchange with Mexico, and has been active in projects helping children in Baja California.

SURFSIDE NISSAN

For well over a half-century Nissan has been building its well-known automobiles, and the public instinctively envisions quality when the name is mentioned.

"It's because we pay attention to details, the basics that others often forget," says Akito Iriyama, Nissan dealer in Oceanside. Surfside Nissan, at 2205 Vista Way, has been in business in Oceanside for many years, first in the downtown area, and later in the El Camino Shopping Center.

Almost a decade ago Iriyama—who is president of Surfside Nissan and a director of its parent company, Saitama Nissan, in Japan—bought the Oceanside firm from two area brothers. In 1981, when Iriyama moved the dealership into its new shopping center quarters, it represented an investment of $2.5 million in the community's future as a budding oceanfront trade and living area for residents of Los Angeles, Orange, and San Diego counties.

Surfside was the first Nissan auto dealer in the United States to be owned

The parts and service staff ensures Surfside Nissan's consistently high ranking in customer satisfaction polls.

outright by a Japanese company, which has advantages for customers since management is able to maintain continuity, consistency, and quality from manufacturing all the way through the various marketing phases into customer services and follow-up activities.

Surfside often ranks first in Southern California in customer satisfaction in polls done by the manufacturer. "We are very sensitive to customer needs," states Iriyama. "We use Japanese sales methods, paying careful attention to small details that really aren't notice-

able at first, but are the basis for long-term customer satisfaction and repeat business. Our philosophy is, 'Do it right the first time.'"

Iriyama has been in the United States a long time, putting down solid roots after enmeshing himself in a new culture, economy, and life-style. Born in Japan, he was educated in Tokyo, graduating from Tamagawa University. He came to the United States when he was 24 years old, after working in Japan as a Nissan mechanic. Nissan sent him to the United States in 1967 to work in a Gardena auto distribution center.

He returned to Japan in 1970 for further work and training, first as a Nissan salesman, going on to become a parts manager, general manager, and then dealer. In 1979 he returned to the United States to ultimately buy the Oceanside dealership for his company.

When acquired, Surfside had only 30 employees and was selling roughly 500 cars per year. Now the company—with 65 employees and an annual payroll of $2.1 million—sells 1,800 new and used cars per year, far above the average for the 1,100 Nissan dealers in America.

"We are different than other auto agencies," says Iriyama. "We are a family of employees, well trained and involved in community activities, with a long-term stake in the community, and thus involved in the destiny of Oceanside. We will be around for a long time."

Surfside Nissan sells 1,800 new and used cars per year, far above the national average for Nissan dealerships. Pictured here are Surfside's salespeople and office staff.

VILLA MARINA HOTEL

The Villa Marina calls itself a hotel, but it really isn't. It is a miniature, out-of-the-way resort—a quiet, little-known place in which to soak up some sun on a long weekend, enjoy the beach, relax, dine at some better-than-average restaurants, and have a little fun.

The Villa Marina is situated on the tip of a peninsula that juts out into the Pacific Ocean from Oceanside Harbor, and every sailboat in or out of the harbor must pass by its front door. And the back door—really a tree-ringed swimming pool and cabana—faces the Pacific Ocean, the waves of which occasionally send clouds of mist into the air.

The ocean sunsets are a spectacular part of the Villa's tradition, and someone is sure to remark, "There's nothing between us and China but water."

Every room is a suite, equipped for more than just an overnight stay. Each has a bedroom, living room with a gas-log fireplace, and fully equipped kitchen.

"Most of our guests stay with us for long periods," says the general manager. "We do have some overnighters, but the majority are here for relaxation, using us as home base for sailing, visits to the zoo, swimming, and trips to Disneyland and Hollywood. Most stay with us about two weeks."

Despite the relative seclusion, the Villa Marina Hotel is still within easy access to theaters, museums, and arts and entertainment attractions of two major metropolitan areas, 45 minutes by car from San Diego and one hour from Los Angeles.

The oceanside site, combining both a placid bay and churning surf, lends an atmosphere to the Villa Marina that has made it an attractive site for beauty pageants and photography contests, and many models have been photographed there. Alongside the hotel is a major restaurant, the Jolly Roger, and boaters tie up their vessels at a dock directly in front of the Villa Marina.

Built in the 1960s, the 57-room ho-

Guests who stay at Oceanside Harbor's Villa Marina Hotel are greeted by a picturesque view of churning surf and sailboats in a placid bay. Featuring a cabana and swimming pool, the 57-suite hotel has all the amenities necessary for long, relaxing visits.

tel is an Oceanside landmark, quickly recognized and easily found. Owned by a group of investors who also operate 37 hotels and motels in the western United States, it is operated by Ha' Penny Management Company.

Business meetings are often held at the Villa Marina Hotel, chosen for its quiet and pleasant surroundings, but more so for its location, a quickly accessible mid-point site for Angelenos and San Diegans entering via Interstate 5—three minutes away—or Amtrak trains that stop nearby at a major transportation center.

"We are truly unique," explains the manager. "There are no more sites like this on the West Coast, and if there were, no one would be allowed to build on them."

HARRY SINGH & SONS

Harry Singh is an Oceanside legend.

His story is the stuff of the American dream: Immigrant farmer becomes successful, quietly helps shape his community, anonymously aids philanthropic causes, becomes a friend of two presidents, and leaves behind a successful farming and land company—a legacy to his children and grandchildren based on honesty, hard work, and fair dealing.

Wearing plaid shirts, work pants, a broad-brimmed hat, and driving a battered old pickup truck containing a dog or two, Singh always looked like a farm worker. Yet he could stop at a phone booth and instantly talk to a congressman or senator as naturally as he sat in the second row at President Ronald Reagan's first inaugural.

In 1982, when Singh died at age 81, the county board of supervisors adjourned in his honor following comments about the "very quiet, very private man of the soil" who was "concerned with a multitude of the area's social and economic problems."

The organization that Singh left behind, still known as Harry Singh & Sons, is a major family-operated farm company in Oceanside that grows crops year-round on several hundred acres across Oceanside, Camp Pendleton, and Bonsall. It has 100 to 500 employees, depending on the season, packs its own produce, and sells it nationwide.

Singh & Sons also owns several pieces of Oceanside property, including a medical center, some acreage under development, and land in New Mexico, most of which was accumulated over the years by Harry.

Harry Singh left his native India at age 16 to attend school in the United States. However, because of his father's death, he was soon forced to go to work. Singh, a math whiz and fluent in several languages, began by keeping books for farmers in Colorado and New Mexico, and was soon operating a truck route selling fruits and vegetables—a route

that expanded into a multistate operation. He married a Taos, New Mexico, girl named Oclides, who was his lifelong companion and ultimately the inspiration for their move to California.

In 1941 Harry and Oclides moved to Oceanside, leased land from the government, and began farming. They grew celery and tomatoes—tomatoes are still the company's principal crop—built their own packing sheds one board at a time, made wooden shipping crates by hand, and did their own delivering.

It apparently was during this hardscrabble time that Harry developed his philosophy of hard work, tending to his crops while building a house for a growing family. Oceanside contemporaries

Harry Singh, Sr., and his wife, Oclides.

say that throughout his life Harry worked 18-hour days, prowling the fields at night and checking temperatures, soil conditions, and irrigation pipes. Said one, "He just generally communed with nature, what we today call exercising hands-on leadership, the necessary ingredient for success in any endeavor."

The labels on Singh's wooden shipping crates were—and remain—visible symbols of his religious faith: a cross atop a glowing halo. A devout Catholic, Singh would kneel regularly and pray with his workers at planting time, a practice that continues to this day.

Several generations of farm workers have been employed by the Singh family, largely because Harry cared for them in both bad and good times,

Discussing farm operations at Stuart Farms Ranch at Camp Pendleton are (from left): Harry Singh, Jr.; Pastor Curiel, foreman (seated); the late Harry Singh; and Ralph Burnette. Photo circa 1975

say his friends and relatives. "One of the reasons we have children and grandchildren of workers still with us is that my grandfather worked with them in the fields, staying in contact, being personally involved in their successes and problems, and listening to them," explains Harry's granddaughter, Luawanna Maria Hallstrom, who has an active role in the company today.

At the time of his death Harry was survived by his wife, Oclides; two sons, Harry Singh, Jr., and Gene; three daughters, Patricia Singh Burnette, Gladys Singh Bergen, and Juanita Singh Dreger; a sister; 13 grandchildren; and two great-grandchildren. A fourth daughter, Banje, died at three months of age.

The business today is managed by family members: Harry's wife, Oclides; Harry Jr.; Gene; and Patricia, with most of the remainder of the family involved in some aspect. All of Harry's descendants live within a few miles of Oceanside.

The firm has continued Harry's political, social, and economic involvement in the community—an involvement that was little known during his lifetime since he was such a private person. But at his funeral, and in bits and pieces that turned up later, it was found that he had aided in building the Oceanside Harbor through his contacts with the federal government, and was a consistent contributor to the Boys' Club, the church, and political causes.

It was through his work for the Republican Party that Harry met and worked with presidents Richard Nixon and Ronald Reagan, occasionally using these friendships to the advantage of Oceanside federal projects.

"It's difficult to estimate how much he did for the community," says John Steiger, a longtime friend and area realtor. "His political influence helped many city projects, and he gave generously and anonymously when a good cause came along."

TRI-CITY MEDICAL CENTER

For one-third of a century the Tri-City Hospital District has quietly been serving the medical needs of San Diego County's north coastal communities. So quietly, in fact, that the average citizen hasn't noticed that it has grown into a major regional medical facility, widely recognized for the depth and variety of its medical and surgical services, as well as for its use of the latest in high-technology medicine.

The need for a hospital in the North County was first expressed in 1952 by the leaders of the chambers of commerce of the three cities—Oceanside, Carlsbad, and Vista—Eugene L. Geil, Chris Christiansen, and C.H. McLean, who formed an organization that led to the creation of the district. Geil and Christiansen were appointed by the county board of supervisors to serve on the first board of directors of the district in 1957.

The now distinguished institution—known as Tri-City Medical Center, a term that better describes the breadth of its activities—serves a quarter-million people in a 120-square-mile area, including the communities of Oceanside, Carlsbad, and Vista, the three cities that form the basis for the medical center's name.

It is an accredited 438-bed, acute-care, not-for-profit facility with 2,100 employees, 450 physicians, 650 members in its auxiliary, and a reputation for being in touch with the community and its needs. Its record of sound, innovative medicine has long been exemplified in the high quality of its emergency department, which treats more than 55,000 patients annually and is the busiest in San Diego County due to its proximity to the Pacific Ocean and growing population.

Just as emergency medicine has expanded over the years to meet the needs of the community, other medical services were initiated to accommodate the senior population in North County. More than half of Tri-City's patients are over the age of 65, and the medical

Five shovels were used to start Tri-City Medical Center in 1959. Pictured (from left) are B.M. Christiansen, Eugene Geil, J.H. Fotheringham, E.S. Ridley, and Mrs. R.E. Ashbrook.

center provides for them with such specialized services as a complete cardiology department—including facilities for open-heart surgery and postoperative rehabilitation—an osteoporosis center, a hospice program, dialysis center, cancer program, day treatment, and home care.

Steady population growth, better highways, and societal changes have brought many thousands of new and younger home-owning couples to the North County, people who commute southward on a daily basis to down-

Tri-City Medical Center now has 438 beds and provides comprehensive medical services for the North County.

town San Diego and northward to Orange County's high-rise offices; this group has caused a new emphasis on pediatrics, neonatology, orthopedics, alternative birthing, and mammography.

Population growth has always been a challenge for the medical center's management. In the first few years after the hospital district was created in 1957, Tri-City's service area experienced a population increase of 32 percent, motivating expansion planning even before the initial 87-bed building was fully occupied. "That is still the story," says Richard A. Hachten, chief executive officer, who administers the district's $165-million annual budget. "Our occupancy rate is often close to 95 percent, and it is a constant challenge to keep buildings and services current with our communities' needs. We continually update our information with demographic studies on which we base strategic planning."

Tri-City Medical Center also operates Oceanview Recovery Center, a 56-bed adult and adolescent chemical dependency facility, a day treatment center in Oceanside, and an outpatient rehabilitation center in Vista. The medical center is currently planning to triple the capacity of its emergency-care facilities, expand its surgical suites and women's services, construct a 200-bed skilled nursing facility, and build a children's day-care center.

DEUTSCH ENGINEERED CONNECTING DEVICES COMPANY

The 170,000-square-foot Deutsch plant in Oceanside employs a work force ranging from assemblers to skilled precision metalworkers, and is considered a stabilizing influence in Oceanside's economy.

For more than two decades the Deutsch Engineered Connecting Devices Company has been a significant economic force in Oceanside. Operating at the Oceanside Municipal Airport, the firm makes a variety of electro-mechanical devices for the defense and aerospace industries.

Headquartered in Banning, it is one of a family of several U.S.- and foreign-affiliated companies owned by Alex Deutsch, an engineering entrepreneur who as a young man started his career by opening a small machine shop.

That was in 1938, and the country was in the midst of the Depression. But Deutsch took the risk, operating with a handful of employees in a rented building in Los Angeles; machined parts were made at night and delivered during the day.

The business gradually grew into a large metal-job shop, and as the Depression ended and America entered World War II, the Deutsch Company became a major supplier of component parts for military aircraft. Diversification followed the end of the war, when Deutsch began making metal consumer goods, including lawn furniture, ballpoint pens, and cigarette lighters.

Further diversification saw the firm abandon consumer goods in favor of small, aircraft-related components, a field in which it is recognized worldwide today.

In 1954 Deutsch purchased the Mono-Watt Connector Division of General Electric, moving it to Huntington Park two years later. By the following year growth necessitated long-range strategic planning, and Deutsch made the bold decision to move manufacturing facilities away from administra-

The Deutsch Family Park, used by Deutsch employees and their families, is an example of the company's commitment to good employee relations.

tive and planning offices. A plant was opened in Beaumont, and subsequently in Banning. The 100,000-square-foot facility opened in Oceanside in 1967 has grown to 170,000 square feet today. The airport was chosen to facilitate shipping, both incoming and outgoing, to other Deutsch plants and to customers nationwide.

Deutsch, one of North County's major employers, has grown beyond the firm's wildest dreams, largely because of its philosophy of dedication to delivering the finest-quality product, on time, and at a fair price. Its work force, ranging from assemblers to highly skilled precision metalworkers, is considered a stabilizing influence in Oceanside's economy.

The parent Deutsch company has four divisions in Southern California, one in New York, and is affiliated with five firms in foreign countries. All produce aircraft-related items, including many small components such as fasteners, hydraulic items, and aircraft tools.

Officials at Deutsch Engineered Connecting Devices Company say the firm's philosophy is founded on a belief that building good employee relations leads to a family atmosphere in the work place, ultimately rewarding both initiative and experience, which together form the basis for future growth.

LAWRENCE/DALEY FAMILIES

The Lawrence and Daley families are part of Oceanside's heritage.

Thomas M. Lawrence, a Texas farmer, settled in Oceanside at the turn of the century and earned a living as a farmer, house painter, and decorator. He was, however, mainly a commercial fisherman and tour boat operator who also dabbled in real estate.

William Edward Daley, a retired South Dakota farmer, and his wife, Anna O'Brien, moved to Oceanside in 1938. Lured here by his two grown daughters (he had seven children altogether) who had settled in Oceanside earlier and had written him letters praising the city, Daley brought his wife and two teenage sons with him.

These two families, later related through marriage, left a legacy in Oceanside and Southern California— one of honest, hardworking descendants who contribute to the moral fiber that holds America together.

Lawrence, or "T.M.," as he was known according to town records, was a skilled paperhanger, house and sign painter, and glazier. But his real love was the sea, where, until the early 1940s, he fished commercially in vessels he built himself, taking fishermen and tourists out and setting lobster traps. In 1903 he married Vera Princess Sanders. Originally from Kentucky, Vera had lived in Escondido, where T.M. would ride his bike each weekend to court her.

He also bought and sold houses and undeveloped land, becoming one of the city's land entrepreneurs. His great-grandson, John A. Daley, is today one of Oceanside's better-known real estate brokers. T.M. also farmed for a few years, and newspaper records indicate that in 1910 he operated a paint and wallpaper store.

In 1919 T.M. became the town's deputy marshal, and the local newspaper recorded his first arrest: Using a stopwatch, he ticketed a motorist for

Captain Jimmy Lawrence (right) proudly displays a marlin caught by John B. Winston (left) whose boat Lawrence captained for many years.

Brothers Gene and Bill Daley operated two filling stations on Hill Street. Pictured is the station on the site that now is home to the Disabled American Veterans Store on South Hill Street.

crossing Second Street at the then-breathtaking speed of 26 miles per hour, which resulted in a five-dollar fine for the driver, a railroad employee.

A history book published in 1915 cited Lawrence for "being among the able and energetic men who are doing much to develop the resources and to call attention to the advantages of Oceanside as a place of interest, and to its natural advantages for business as well as pleasure."

T.M. and Vera had 10 children— Thelma, Betty June, Birdie May, Vera Alice, Hazel, James, Howard, Evelyn, Billie, and Walter—none of whom currently live in Oceanside.

Their daughter, Thelma Garrigan, operated Garrigan's, a well-known Oceanside night club on Third and Tremont streets, from the 1930s until the early 1940s, when it was bought by the government and converted into a

USO for men and women in the service.

A United Press dispatch of August 28, 1931, credits T.M.'s son James with saving the lives of 18 people on a water taxi he operated. An injured Captain James Lawrence battled flames from a gas vapor explosion to secure life preservers for his passengers, all of whom leaped into the sea and were later rescued.

James married Thelma Hughes, who has been an Oceanside resident since 1921. He built and operated his own commercial fishing boats until his death in 1947.

Interestingly, Thelma's sister, Georgia, married William Reid Couts, great-grandson of Cave Couts, one of Oceanside's earliest, most colorful, and influential citizens. He owned Rancho Guajome and thousands of acres in the San Luis Rey Valley. Georgia lived until 1975, and William "Bill" Couts lives

At a 1911 family reunion in Texas are T.M. and Vera Lawrence (standing, second and third from right, respectively), and four of their children: Hazel, Jimmy, Howard (second row, second, third, and fourth from left, respectively), and Walter (bottom row, second from left).

in Long Beach.

James and Thelma had two daughters, Dolly Louise and Linda Lee. Linda, a lifelong Oceanside resident, is married to James Randall, with whom she has three children, Laurie Martha, James Wayne, and Shelly Lee.

William Daley and his wife, Anna O'Brien, arrived in Oceanside in 1938. They believed they were distant relatives of the late Chicago mayor, Richard Daley. Already a retired farmer when he arrived, William worked for a short time as an assembler during World War II at the Consolidated Aircraft plant in San Diego.

Anna O'Brien was born in Decorah, Iowa, on April 25, 1884, and William Edward began life in Brodhead, Wisconsin, on May 11, 1886. They were married on January 8, 1908, and farmed in Miller, South Dakota. These good Irish Catholics had seven children: Mary Ethel, Helen Elizabeth, Edward John, Raymond Andrew, Vivian Catharine, William Francis, and Eugene Bernard. Vivian and Eugene presently reside in Oceanside.

World War II veteran Eugene, the youngest, is today a prominent real estate broker. He is married to Dolly

Louise Lawrence, with whom he has had eight children, all of whom are living in Southern California as productive, community-oriented citizens. James Lawrence Daley is a real estate developer and loan broker; John Allan Daley, a real estate broker, Oceanside historian, amateur photographer, and businessman; Maureen Daley Wieland publishes *Trader* magazines covering Orange County; Nancy Lee Anderson is an Orange County magazine publisher; Julie Louise Leffard, is a company office manager; Erin Kathleen Beitner is a college student majoring in communications; and Jennifer Keese is a graduate student.

Eugene and his brother, Bill, who was a well-known Oceanside insurance agent, started the city's first private security patrol. For several years afterward they operated Daley Bros. Brake and Wheel Service at two locations on Hill Street.

Bill and his wife, Geraldine Nadon, who passed away in 1984, had five children. Bill died in 1970.

Helen Daley McIntyre was the first Daley to come to Oceanside. After vacationing there, she made the permanent move in 1936. Shortly afterward, she married Bert McIntyre, originally from Arizona, and had three children. Helen died in 1986.

Vivian Daley Bricker followed her sister, with whom she later lured their father, mother, and two youngest brothers to California. She still lives in Oceanside with her husband, Don. She retired a few years ago from her job as an escrow officer for the Oceanside branch of the Bank of America, a career that spanned 30 years and one that has become nearly synonymous with the Daley name: the real estate industry.

With the addition of 15 grandchildren and numerous cousins, nieces, and nephews, the Lawrence/Daley family will continue to maintain and enhance their proud heritage as well as continue their valuable contributions to their communities.

NORTH COUNTY TRANSIT DISTRICT

As villages and small towns grow into cities, and in turn evolve into people-packed metropolitan areas, the residents traditionally become acutely aware of the necessity for public transportation, for leaving the driving to train and bus operators.

Nowhere is that philosophy better expressed than in North San Diego County, where the people in an area of more than 1,000 square miles—and including eight cities—have banded together to solve its people-moving problems.

That solution is the North County Transit District, which has its roots in a massive linkup of city, rural, and small-town bus services. In the past decade the NCTD has emerged as a respected regional government agency that not only provides quality bus service but is also currently expanding into express commuter bus service and express commuter rail transportation.

Because North County's population has exploded during the past two decades, its new home owners remembered bigger cities with heavy traffic and congested streets, and expressed a desire to protect the open spaces, the decidedly lower noise levels, and improved air quality. They supported a public transportation system that long ago outgrew an inaccurate image that buses are only for the poor, the young, and the elderly.

Social mobility, environmental protection, and energy conservation were key factors underlying a 1971 state statute that annually provides funds to assist local public transportation efforts, recognizing that such systems as the NCTD are an important aspect of twenty-first century living. The old concept that the system must be supported from the bus fare boxes was tossed out alongside the jocular concept that every Californian had a birthright that included a set of car keys and a designated slot on the freeways.

Today the North County Transit District carries 8 million passengers per year—roughly 30,000 a day—on 26 bus routes serving the cities of Oceanside, Escondido, Vista, Carlsbad, San Marcos, Del Mar, Solana Beach, Encinitas, and communities in an unincorporated area of the county. On an annual budget of about $20 million, its directors—all of whom are residents of these cities—serve the coastal area between Orange County and La Jolla, and inland to the Pala Indian Reservation and south of Escondido.

The transit district's next big goal is to operate fast commuter trains between Oceanside and San Diego, followed by train service from Oceanside inland to Escondido. Both plans would generally improve North County living by relieving freeway congestion, lowering noise and frustration levels, and

conserving energy.

The impetus for forming the regional district came from California Senator Jim Mills and the introduction of Senate Bill 101, which would have formed a single transit agency for San Diego County. North County cities, believing their interests would be better served by having their own district, banded together behind Senate Bill 802. This legislation, passed in 1976, created the North San Diego County Transit Development Board and merged the existing Oceanside City Transit and Escondido City Transit into one coordinated service area.

The North County Transit District has its headquarters in Oceanside, a large maintenance facility in the San Luis Rey Valley, and a subheadquarters in Escondido. A major transportation center is planned for Escondido, comparable to the one in Oceanside.

District directors believe that the big white buses with the yellow and blue stripes are indeed the nucleus of the North County's transportation system of the future.

The North County Transit District serves the cities of Oceanside, Vista, San Marcos, Carlsbad, Del Mar, Escondido, Solana Beach, Encinitas, and communities in an unincorporated area of the county. Shown is a bus parked at The Oceanside Transit Center, a multimodal transit center for the coastal area. The organization's offices are located nearby at 311 South Tremont.

LEISURE TECHNOLOGY

In the waning years of the twentieth century, older Americans have emerged as a dynamic new force. These people are significantly different from previous generations in that they are far healthier than their parents; more vigorous, with a zest for life; and they are considerably more prosperous and better prepared for retirement. Many own their own homes and enjoy a discretionary income that comprises nearly 30 percent of the nation's spending.

No longer content merely to save and build estates for their children, the age 55-plus generation views retirement as an opportunity to begin an exciting, new life, initiating new careers and varied leisure pursuits that include political activities and social concerns.

As Oceanside grew so did its new older and more sophisticated population. In 1979 a major development firm began to meet the needs of this new demographic group.

Leisure Technology, the largest national producer of retirement communities for active adults, began work on Leisure Village Ocean Hills in Oceanside, adjacent to Cannon Road. Today 900 homes are completed and another 750 are in various stages of construction.

The decidedly upscale villa homes constitute a suburban resort, a master-planned community of Aegean architecture built around large, green, open spaces with structural amenities that enhance the quality of life. Cultural facilities include a theater auditorium for concerts, banquet dining, and chamber music recitals. Recreational facilities include photography labs, ceramics and woodworking studios, health clubs, a swimming pool, spa, and a large golf course.

Leisure Technology was founded 30 years ago in New Jersey on the principle that active retired people want more than just another retirement community. Its original 5,000-unit Leisure Village in Ocean County, New Jersey, was so successful that the company

subsequently finished three more major projects in the same seashore area and a fourth in a nearby county.

Today the firm has sold more than 16,000 homes and has major communities—in addition to New Jersey—in New York, Florida, Illinois, and California. It is a publicly held company listed on the New York Stock Exchange.

"Our success has been based on the fact that we meet the needs of America's new [older] adults who are more sophisticated and more active than past generations," explains Joseph A. Gallagher, president of the Southern California division. "Leisure Technology anticipated these changes in the market and installed more extensive amenities, cultural support activities, and health facilities."

Among Leisure Village Ocean Hills' amenities is Ocean Hills Country Club.

Leisure Technology has developed Leisure Village Ocean Hills in Oceanside, adjacent to Cannon Road, for today's more active retired generation.

The firm entered the California market in 1975 to develop Leisure Village in Ventura County, which the company says was one of its most successful ventures. It was completed in 1984. Leisure Technology has also begun family housing development with projects in Oceanside, Escondido, and Carlsbad.

One of the reasons for Leisure Technology's success, the company believes, is its strategy of long-term community involvement. Gallagher is an Oceanside Chamber of Commerce director, and the firm is a major supporter of the Oceanside Women's Resource Center, has underwritten various community concerts, and was a contributor to the community's Rose Parade float.

COLLINS DEVELOPMENT COMPANY

For a quarter-century the Collins companies have developed land in San Diego, building homes, apartments, shopping centers, and industrial buildings. The group of four firms constitutes one of San Diego's largest developers, doing $50 million to $60 million a year of contracting, well over $20 million annually in developing new properties, while managing a $400-million portfolio of real estate.

Serving as the parent organization is Collins Development Company, founded in 1962 by Harry A. Collins, a Stanford University graduate in engineering who went on to build more than 2 million square feet of structures in the nation's seventh-largest city and carve out a position of stature in the community for himself and his enterprises.

Its subsidiaries are Collins General Contractors, the construction side of the operation; Collins Asset Management Group, which uses a sophisticated computer to coordinate its property portfolio; and Collins Rancho Del Oro, a 2,000-acre community being master-planned in Oceanside for completion within 10 years.

The ventures consist of a series of partnerships owned by Harry A. Collins, E. Tyler Miller, Jr., Robert A. Stine, and William A. Tribolet. Each are active in the day-to-day operation of the group, placing a high value on such participation—which gives the firm the ability to react quickly to shifts in the market, problems, and opportunities.

The TMI, a division of Nytronics, building.

In the early years the firm was largely a residential builder in La Jolla, Rancho Santa Fe, and Lomas Santa Fe, and in 1970 added industrial development and neighborhood shopping centers. In 1980 Collins General Contractors was formed as a separate entity to continue to do in-house building and to become a more competitive force in the construction business. Two-thirds of its contracts are currently for outside clients.

The property management organization is one of the largest, most tightly

Rancho Del Oro Technology Park.

controlled operations in San Diego, and its computer-guided management is able to maintain a level of quality and responsiveness that corporate officers believe cannot be matched at competitive prices.

In the past 15 years the company has developed more than 5 million square feet of industrial, research and development, and office space, and it is likely to be long remembered in the community for its Rancho Del Oro project in Oceanside. The first phase is a 470-acre technical/industrial park. Plans call for a mixed-use community, including shopping centers, housing, and the other amenities that make up an oceanfront community near two densely populated major metropolitan areas.

Over the years Collins Development Company has had successful joint-venture operations with such major institutions as Aetna Life Insurance, Connecticut Mutual Life, Home Federal Savings, the San Diego Housing Authority, and Great American Savings.

DAVID RORICK

Every community has had its leaders, usually a small group who, because of their abilities or their economic position in the community, have led community endeavors. They initiate change through suggestion, logic, and reason, passing on their quest for a higher quality of life for all to succeeding generations by their roles in such important endeavors as improving education, building libraries and churches, installing waterworks, creating jobs, and raising children who will emulate the same selfless community service as their parents.

The Rorick family of Oceanside is one such family, having helped to shape the city since just after the turn of the century, when Oceanside was a tiny dry-farming village by the sea and horse-drawn carriages were beginning to give way to the self-powered, "horseless carriage."

The first Rorick in Oceanside was David, a young Iowa attorney—and the son of a lawyer—who came by way of Missouri and Texas, sent to Oceanside in 1905 to look after a relative's interest in the First National Bank. In 1906 he bought two lots on South Pacific Street and settled with his wife, Vinnie, and two daughters, Helen and Ruth, at 110 South Pacific.

David's father was an Ohio native, as well as an officer in the Union Army

in the Civil War, a member of the Kansas Legislature, and a top executive at a national insurance company. Becoming acquainted with California while settling damage claims following the San Francisco Earthquake, he moved to Oceanside upon his retirement in 1913, taking up residence at 108 South Pacific, next door to his son.

The younger Rorick set the pattern for generations to come, practicing law and serving on the city council for two terms, 1910 to 1912, and 1914 to 1916. He was city attorney from 1924 to 1926, and he and his wife, Vinnie, twice served terms on the library board. He was also a director of the Oceanside Building and Loan Association.

The Roricks had three children, Helen, Ruth, and a son—David Rorick, Jr., born in Oceanside. Helen married William S. McGill, a walnut grower-rancher, and Ruth married Clarence A. Stevens, a banker and rancher.

David married Maureen McInerny, who held a bachelor's degree from Dominican College in San Rafael and a master's degree from Stanford. It is David Jr., now 75 years old, who is the current patriarch of the Roricks, as well as a community leader.

A graduate of Pomona College, he has been active in civic and business affairs nearly all his life, a shaper of public opinion, influential in politics, and a

patrician member of the city's Old Guard.

His main business through the years has been Rorick Buick, a car dealership he opened in 1941. But the list of his community activities overshadows any economic enterprise. He was chairman of the Oceanside Planning Commission, a director of the national Audubon Society, chairman of the Oceanside Library Board, director of the San Diego County Water Authority, president of the chamber of commerce, an Exalted Ruler of the Elks Lodge, president of the Rotary Club, a founder of the Boys' Club, director of Oceanside Federal Savings & Loan Association, a director of the Museum of Natural History, founder of the North County Concert Association, and a member of the city's Water and Sewer Comity.

David Jr. and Maureen had four children: David III, Nicholas, Clare, and Sarah. David III is a San Diego State University graduate associated with a San Francisco group assisting Central Americans to secure U.S. citizenship; Nicholas is a medical doctor practicing in Pennsylvania; Clare, who held a doctorate in French, married Gregory Athens; and Sarah, a Stanford graduate, married Richard Orlando. Clare died in 1987.

THE JOHN A. STEIGER FAMILY

The Steiger name was first heard in Oceanside in 1888, when George and Hedwig Steiger settled in San Luis Rey Valley and visited the "ocean side."

In 1919 their oldest son, John Paul, married Laura Marron, daughter of Juan Maria Marron and Lorenza Serrano, whose grandparents in 1842 were grantees of the 13,311-acre Rancho Agua Hedionda land grant where Carlsbad and Vista Way are today. He and Laura had five children: John Anthony, Doris, Helen, Alice Lorraine, and Robert. John P. operated large tractors on Rancho Santa Margarita y Las Flores. During the Depression he was a city engineering inspector and Water Department foreman. While working under cold, damp conditions, he was fatally stricken with pneumonia.

Mary and John Steiger at the 1988 City of Oceanside Centennial Ball. As distinguished members of the Oceanside community, the Steigers have led many organizations and have received several honors for their community involvement.

His oldest child, John A., was 13 years old.

His widow, Laura, a graduate of Oceanside High (1913) and Kelsey-Jenney College (1915), and her young family became a success story of family teamwork from dressmaking and baby-sitting, to magazine, newspaper, and milk routes, washing store windows, sweeping floors, hoeing weeds in lima bean and flower bulb fields, and ushering at the Palomar Movie Theatre.

John A. graduated from Oceanside High in 1937 and went to work for Bank of America until World War II. (He later graduated from Stanford University.) Doris began a career in 1941 with PacTel after graduating from Oceanside-Carlsbad College, retiring in 1982 as an area operations administrator. Helen received teaching degrees from UCLA and Stanford, retiring in 1979. Lorraine "Toddy" graduated from Oceanside-Carlsbad College and is now a semiretired art dealer. Robert, who graduated from the University of California at Davis, is now an agricultural consultant.

During World War II John was commissioned a lieutenant pilot in the Army Air Corps. After the war he became a realtor, serving north San Diego County and establishing the firm of John A. Steiger & Associates. He is a founder and 1946 charter president of the Oceanside-Carlsbad Junior Chamber of Commerce, president of the Oceanside Young Republicans and North San Diego County Young G.O.P., a member of the California Delegation to the 1948 Republican National Convention at Philadelphia, and president of the Oceanside-Carlsbad Realty Board and Oceanside Board of Realtors. In addition, John was named Outstanding Young Man of the Year in 1951 by the Jaycees.

The present Steiger Realtors building was built in 1951 at 709-711 Third Street, across from city hall.

John met Mary Joetta Owens from Oklahoma in 1953. They were married

in June at Old Mission San Luis Rey. They have three children, Laura (University of San Francisco), John Damian (Cal Poly University, Pomona), and Mrs. Susan Steiger Maguire (Washington State University).

John was elected to the San Diego County Republican Central Committee in 1954. He also served as chairman of the City Planning Commission and founder-president of the Greater San Luis Rey Area Planning Council. He organized the Oceanside Yacht Club in 1963 and was 1964 commodore. He was 1966 chamber of commerce president and was elected to the city council in 1968, winning in all precincts. From 1968 to 1972 he was vice-mayor and vice-president of the Oceanside Harbor Board. He was also elected chairman of the San Diego County Comprehensive Planning Organization, now SANDAG. John was one of the community leaders responsible for building Oceanside Harbor, the 18-hole El Camino Country Club and Oceanside Municipal Golf courses, the Palomar and Oceanside airports, and the Bicentennial Heritage Village Park near the historic San Luis Rey Mission. He was largely responsible for saving the 569-acre Guajome Regional Park for Oceanside and Vista. He supported the dedication of the 59-acre Center City Park. He was chairman, Military Affairs Committee, and six-year member of the Advisory Board of the Auto Club of Southern California; 1983 Oceanside Rotary Club president; and 1987 co-founder of Leadership 2000.

John's wife, Mary, was honored by the International Conference of Christians and Jews, and in 1977 was the first woman elected president of the Oceanside Chamber of Commerce. She was named 1984 Realtor of the Year and from 1982 to 1984 she served as founder and board chairman of the First National Bank North County. The *Blade-Tribune* named Mary 1981 Oceanside Citizen of the Year and John 1985 Oceanside Citizen of the Year.

THE ROSICRUCIAN FELLOWSHIP

For more than three quarters of a century the world headquarters of The Rosicrucian Fellowship has been an Oceanside landmark.

The dome of the big, white Rosicrucian Temple on a bluff overlooking the San Luis Rey Valley is the highly visible symbol of an association of Christian mystics who arrived in Oceanside shortly after the turn of the century.

On the 40-acre retreat, known as Mount Ecclesia, is a large administration building, the Temple, a Guest House that houses a library and classrooms, small chapel, and a printing and publishing plant. A landscaped meditation path along a canyon rim leads to a healing center. Prayers for the world's sick have been said every day since 1911.

Through the years the Fellowship has often been called an island of tranquility in the city, but never more so than in recent years, when its once-rural Mission Avenue site became surrounded by the urban sprawl of a fast-growing metropolitan area.

Although the Fellowship is in the city, it is a decidedly pastoral-like world, removed from the hustle and bustle of urban life. This oasis, curiously, also reflects the philosophical position of the Fellowship itself regarding the secular world.

In their mission of teaching, healing, and ministry, Fellowship members are very much out in the world. But their intense belief in the doctrine of rebirth supports their conviction that man is progressing toward a higher plane of existence than his present physical life. Geared toward service to others, the Fellowship is very much a Christian group, using its philosophy and the Bible as a bridge to bring science and religion closer together.

The group has thousands of members worldwide and study centers in many major cities. It conducts classes on religion, the Bible, philosophy, and spiritual astrology in Oceanside and by correspondence throughout the world, and publishes a monthly magazine, *Rays From the Rose Cross,* for students, members, and the public.

The Rosicrucian Fellowship has its roots in the teachings of a fourteenth-century philosopher named Christian Rosenkreuz, translatable as Christian Rose Cross, hence the organization's symbol of seven red roses emblazoned on a white Christian cross. The Rosicrucian Fellowship was founded in 1911 by Max Heindel, a devotee of Esoteric Christianity, and is a broad, mystical movement holding that special revelations have been made to selected individuals by higher beings on higher planes of existence to provide mankind with spiritual guidance. Heindel was given a revelation in Germany by a Brother of the Order of the Rose Cross that resulted in his writing the *Rosicrucian Cosmo-Conception,* a book laying down the Fellowship's basic tenets. Af-

ter publication of the book, Heindel lectured in various U.S. cities prior to establishing in Oceanside the international headquarters of a rapidly growing association.

In addition to following Rosicrucian precepts that mandate spreading the word of Esoteric Christianity, strength of character, honesty, compassion, healing, courage, self-reliance, and selfless service, Probationers must also take vows of vegetarianism and abstain from alcohol, smoking, and illicit drugs.

A vital part of the Rosicrucian philosophy lies in the study of the Bible, spiritual astrology, and spiritual healing. Mount Ecclesia's healing department building has a cross-shape floor plan, with a chapel at the center of the two arms; the roof has a stained-glass skylight with the symbols of a five-pointed star in the center.

The Fellowship takes pride in the fact it has no permanent appointed leader. Routine worldly matters are handled by a nine-member board of trustees elected to three-year terms by the membership.

Visitors are welcome, and may attend devotional services at the chapel, visit the bookstore, and attend classes when in session.

The Rosicrucian Fellowship's Oceanside visitor information center and bookstore.

THE FIELDSTONE COMPANY

The Fieldstone Company was founded in May 1981 by Peter M. Ochs. In eight years it has become one of the major home builders in Southern California. Ochs, who is president and chairman of the board, is assisted by chief operating officer Keith A. Johnson, senior vice-president and Orange County Division manager David R. Langlois, and a staff of more than 120 dedicated employees.

In its first year of operation The Fieldstone Company constructed 81 single-family, detached homes for a sales total of $10.4 million. In 1987 total sales were $200 million with nearly 1,200 homes built.

Fieldstone attributes its rapid development and success in part to the fact that it stresses traditional values that include integrity and excellence. One of its goals is to construct quality homes at affordable prices, keeping in mind knowledge of market conditions and consumer tastes. Within a well-defined organizational structure, dedi-

The Fieldstone Company executives include (left to right) Peter M. Ochs, president; Keith A. Johnson, chief operating officer; and David R. Langlois, senior vice-president.

cated and experienced personnel give careful attention to detail, providing assurance that the standards that have been set are kept.

Realizing the impact made on the community by a home builder and resolving to act as a responsible community citizen, the company established The Fieldstone Foundation in 1983, a nonprofit organization that would facilitate distribution of charitable funds in four areas: education and community, cultural, humanitarian, and Christian ministries. All employees are encouraged to suggest charities for the company's support. To date the recipients of its substantial charitable donations include the City of Hope Medical Center in Los Angeles, The Globe Theatre in San Diego, the San Diego Museum of Art, Orangewood (Orange County shelter for abused children), SAY San Diego, Children's Hospital of Orange County, the Laguna Art Museum, the Orange County Performing Arts Center, and South Coast Repertory. Ochs served as president of the South Coast Repertory board of trustees during the 1984-1985 season. In 1980 he was named Man of the Year for Orange County by the City of Hope

One of the foremost builders in Southern California, Fieldstone's belief in quality homes is evidenced in this Rancho Penasquitos model in San Diego.

Medical Center.

In 1985 Fieldstone made a conscious decision to develop a collection of artwork with a historical perspective—paintings that depict the region of Southern California as it was. The Fieldstone Collection now has nearly 150 paintings, which span the 70-year period from 1900 to 1970. The paintings, primarily by California Impressionist artists, provide a beautiful record of the unique geographical area that is Southern California. The collection is displayed in the Fieldstone offices in Newport Beach, in San Diego, and in Brea. In 1985 and in 1987 the Orange County Business Committee for the Arts gave special recognition to The Fieldstone Company for its commitment to the visual and performing arts.

It is clear to see that The Fieldstone Company has in only a few years established itself as a leader in the Southern California business community.

BLADE-TRIBUNE

"Anyone in North County with a community problem knows that he or she can come to the newspaper and, if the cause is legitimate, the *Blade-Tribune* will get involved," says Tom Missett, publisher.

The scrappy, often controversial *Blade-Tribune* has been involved in community affairs in Oceanside since the turn of the century.

Through several different editors and publishers the paper has disseminated news that has not only kept the public informed, but has led and shaped public opinion on every strategic issue impacting the community's social, political, military, agricultural, and economic affairs, as well as on such day-to-day problems as the coast's ever-burgeoning growth, its need for water, and problems with crime, beach erosion and traffic.

"We are not afraid to take on the establishment, to lead people into frank discussions of issues—discussions that could ultimately result in public pressure for change," says Missett, publisher of the newspaper serving the coastal area between San Clemente and Del Mar.

The paper's roots go back to a weekly newspaper, the *Oceanside Blade,* which served what was essentially a small farming community in the early 1900s. A then-relatively new, competing daily, the *Oceanside Tribune* was merged with the *Blade* in 1929, when both papers were bought by Paul and Harold Beck, two young men fresh out of Stanford University who came from an Iowa newspaper family. Circulation of the new *Oceanside Blade-Tribune* was 2,500.

For the next 25 years the Becks operated the paper, selling it in 1954 for $500,000 to Tom Braden, a former federal government official and author of *Eight is Enough* who later became a television commentator in Washington, D.C.

Thirteen years later, in 1967, Howard Publications, which owns 17 daily newspapers and cable television firms, bought the paper for $2.1 million. The paper then had 6,500 subscribers.

Howard Publications, which has operated the paper for more than two decades, has put many millions of dollars into the paper in both talent and equipment through the years, resulting

Tom Missett, publisher.

in the paper's broadened outlook as the area grew in population. Today, under Missett's guidance, the *Blade-Tribune* has dropped "Oceanside" from its masthead, symbolizing its regional editorial approach and a circulation of more than 40,000.

"We are a local paper and that will never change," says Missett. "But local now means intense coverage of all our neighboring communities. And—in ascending order—we attach great significance to county, regional, state, and national news."

The *Blade-Tribune* is the flagship paper that also publishes the *San Dieguito Citizen,* the *La Costan,* the *Del Mar Citizen,* and *Camp Pendleton's Scout.* With two shoppers' newspapers filling niches, the *Blade-Tribune* offers its advertisers 90-percent penetration

For years the Blade-Tribune *has kept the public informed on day-to-day problems and key issues. The paper has recently increased the size of its building and has modernized much of its equipment.*

of the north coastal market.

The paper recently invested $8 million in the future by increasing the size of its building at 1722 South Hill, and by installing new presses, a computerized billing system, telephone system, and mail room equipment.

Much to the chagrin of North County government agencies, the *Blade-Tribune* has long been known as a staunch defender of the First Amendment and the people's right to know. "Our paper is seen as the little man's equalizer," says Missett. "We just don't roll over on issues of knowledge about government affairs, whether it's city hall, a hospital, or the county government."

PATRONS

The following individuals, companies, and organizations have made a valuable commitment to the quality of this publication. Windsor Publications and the Oceanside Historical Society gratefully acknowledge their participation in *Oceanside: Crest of the Wave.*

Best Western Marty's Valley Inn*
Blade-Tribune*
Collins Development Company*
Daley Family*
Deutsch Engineered Connecting Devices
 Company*
The Fieldstone Company*
Lawrence/Daley Families*
Leisure Technology*
The Lightfoot Planning Group*
MiraCosta College*
North County Transit District*
David Rorick*
The Rosicrucian Fellowship*
Harry Singh & Sons*
The John A. Steiger Family*
Surfside Nissan*
Tri-City Medical Center*
Villa Marina Hotel*

*Partners in Progress of *Oceanside: Crest of the Wave.* The histories of these companies and organizations appear in Chapter 6, beginning on page 103.

BIBLIOGRAPHY

BOOKS AND MANUSCRIPTS

Barnard, Harriet. *Oceanside 1769-1945.* Oceanside Public Library, 1969.

Coyer, Richard Joseph. "Cave Johnson Couts: On Both Sides of the Law." *La Campana De Escuela,* vol. 1, no. 1. San Diego: University of San Diego, 1974.

Crouch, Herbert. *Reminiscences of Herbert Crouch, 1869-1915.* San Diego Public Library, 1965.

Davis, Harold B. "The Depression Years." Unpublished manuscript. Oceanside: 1975.

——————. "History of the Oceanside Police Department." Unpublished manuscript. Oceanside: 1975.

Englehardt, Zephiryn. *San Luis Rey, King of the Missions.* J.H. Barry, 1921.

Frazee, W.D. *Oceanside, The Gateway to All of San Diego County.* Oceanside: 1888.

Guinn, J.M. *Historical and Biographical Record of Southern California.* Chicago: Chapman Publishing Company, 1902.

——————. *A History of California and an Extended History of Well Known Citizens of the Past and Present.* Los Angeles: Historic Record Company, 1907.

Oceanside Chamber of Commerce. *Oceanside, Where Life is Worth Living.* Oceanside: 1923.

——————. *Oceanside, Where Life is Worth Living.* Oceanside: 1931.

——————. *Where the Mercury Never Goes Crazy.* Oceanside: 1953.

Oceanside Diamond Jubilee Corporation. *Oceanside Diamond Jubilee 1883-1958.* Oceanside: 1958.

Tac, Pablo. *Indian Life and Customs at Mission San Luis Rey.* Originally written in 1835. Edited and translated by Minna and Gordon Hewes. Old Mission San Luis Rey, California: 1958.

Wayne, John T. "A History of the Oceanside Fire Department." Unpublished manuscript on file at the Oceanside Fire Department. Oceanside: 1977.

Weese, Robert A. "Oceanside Water History." Unpublished manuscript on file at the Oceanside Water and Sewer Department. Oceanside: 1959.

NEWSPAPERS

Oceanside Blade 1892-1929
Oceanside Blade-Tribune 1929-1988
Oceanside Olive Leaf 1896
San Diego Herald
San Diego Union
South Oceanside Diamond 1888-1891

INDEX

GENERAL INDEX
Italicized numbers indicate illustrations.